BETWEEN
THE TESTAMENTS

D. S. RUSSELL

SCM PRESS LTD
BLOOMSBURY STREET LONDON

334 00095 5
FIRST PUBLISHED 1960
REVISED EDITION 1963
SECOND IMPRESSION 1966
THIRD IMPRESSION 1970
FOURTH IMPRESSION 1974
FIFTH IMPRESSION 1976

© SCM PRESS LTD 1960, 1963

PRINTED IN GREAT BRITAIN BY
FLETCHER AND SON LTD
NORWICH

To
Marion, Helen and Douglas

Contents

PART TWO

THE APOCALYPTISTS

Preface

IN most Bibles the period between the Old and the New Testaments is represented by a single blank page which, perhaps, has symbolic significance. 'From Malachi to Matthew' has for long remained vague and unfamiliar to many readers of the Scriptures. Many mysteries remain, but in recent times much light has been cast on this whole period. Exciting new insights have been given by the writings of numbers of scholars and by some remarkable archaeological discoveries.

Early in the present century Dr R. H. Charles wrote much on the subject, and the publication in 1914 of his little book, *Religious Development between the Old and the New Testaments*, introduced a wider reading public to this field of study and helped greatly to fill in the gap in people's understanding of it. But no one could foresee that this period was yet to become a focus of attention not only for scholars but also for 'the man in the street'. The discovery of the Dead Sea Scrolls caught the popular imagination and engaged the attention of world-wide scholarship. These writings are of the utmost importance not only for the account they give of the beliefs and practices of the Covenanters of Qumran, but also for the new interest and knowledge which they bring to the whole inter-testamental period.

In this small volume an attempt is made to review these years in the light of recent study and discoveries and in particular to assess the religious contribution made by that rather strange company of men known as 'the apocalyptists'. Many other subjects relevant to this inter-testamental period might have been dealt with, but the purpose of this book is selective rather than exhaustive, indicating the part which the apocalyptists had to play within the religious development of Judaism and in the preparation of men's minds for the coming of Christianity.

It is hoped that this brief treatment will whet the reader's appetite for more and that he will pursue these studies still further with the help of the bibliography provided.

D. S. RUSSELL

The College,
Rawdon, Leeds
1959

Part One

THE CULTURAL AND LITERARY
BACKGROUND

I

Judaism versus Hellenism

THE years 200 B.C.-A.D. 100, referred to generally as 'the inter-testamental period', are of fundamental importance both for Christianity and for rabbinical Judaism because it was during these centuries that, in a very special sense, the way was being prepared for the emergence of these two great religious faiths. The purpose of this book is to examine, albeit in outline, the culture and literature of these momentous years and to consider the development of certain religious beliefs whose influence was to be felt particularly within the growing Christian Church.

Throughout the whole of this period the Jews were surrounded by Greek culture and civilization and, particularly in the Dispersion, many had to adopt the Greek language either as their only language or as an alternative to their Aramaic tongue. It was inevitable that they should be influenced, and influenced deeply, by the Hellenistic environment in which they lived; the surprising thing is that their response to it was not much greater and that, despite the pressure brought to bear upon them, they were able to maintain their distinctive Jewish faith.

At intervals during the period 170 B.C.-A.D. 70 Jewish nationalism played a most important part in resisting the inroads of

Hellenism. As we shall see, this nationalism was motivated not by political aims only, but also by religious ideals springing from a deep piety on the part of many and rooted in strong theological convictions. For Judaism unlike Hellenism represented not so much a way of life as a national religious movement. Dr F. C. Burkitt, writing of the Judaism of these two and a half centuries, describes it as 'an alternative to Civilization as then understood'. Not only was it *an* alternative, it was *the* alternative, for in the belief of many it would lead men at last to the Kingdom of God whose coming would usher in the New Age of God's appointing.

I. THE RISE AND SPREAD OF HELLENISM

A. *Greeks and Romans*

The word 'Hellenism' is commonly used to describe the civilization of the three centuries or so from the time of Alexander the Great (336-323 B.C.) during which the influence of Greek culture was felt in both East and West. It was the cherished desire of this ruler to found a world-wide Empire bound together in a unity of language, custom and civilization and, in his great military conquests, he did much to realize this idea. After his death, when his Empire in the East was divided between the Seleucids in Syria and the Ptolemies in Egypt, the process of Hellenization continued apace in the countries over which they ruled.

From a very early stage the Jews must have felt the impact of this culture upon their manner of life and particularly upon their religion. Apart from a comparatively small area round about Jerusalem they were not a State but rather a Dispersion, scattered not only throughout Palestine but in every part of the Empire. They were especially open to the influence of Hellenism through the medium of commerce and trade. It was the policy of Alexander and his successors to send Greek colonists in the train of their armies and to plant them as traders in conquered lands. In these lands, particularly in the East, would be many Jews who had been exiled from Palestine many years before and others who, even before the time of Alexander, had emigrated and settled in Greek cities further west. Jewish communities were soon to be found in such places as Syria, Antioch, Damascus, Asia Minor, Macedonia, Greece, Cyprus, Cyrene and Rome. Wherever they were, under Seleucid or Ptolemaic rule, they had for a long time enjoyed the blessings of religious liberty under a policy of religious toleration which would no doubt leave them open to the subtle influence of the Hellenistic culture. The Romans in their turn continued to encourage the development of this culture, especially in the Eastern provinces, and sought by this means to realize the dreams of Alexander the Great. In this regard there was no real break between the Greek and the Roman régimes or, indeed, between the years B.C. and the years A.D. The Hellenistic culture and civilization were characteristic of the whole Graeco-Roman period and it is against this broad historical and cultural background that we are to study the reactions of the Jewish people and their religious faith.

B. *The Septuagint and Hellenistic literature*

From an early date there were Jewish settlements in Egypt, and Alexandria soon won for itself an honoured name, particularly as a literary centre. It was here that the Septuagint translation of the Scriptures into the Greek tongue emerged for the use of Greek-speaking Jews in Egypt who were no longer able to read Hebrew and for whom the translations given in the synagogue services were proving inadequate. The translation of the 'Torah' or Pentateuch took place probably during the reign of Ptolemy II (285-247 B.C.), the name 'Septuagint' being extended later to cover other parts of the Old Testament as well. In the *Letter of*

Aristeas, which at a later date accompanied the Greek Bible, there is a legend that the Septuagint was the result of a royal command of Ptolemy II of Egypt who gave the task of translation into the hands of 72 'elders'. In later forms of the story the number is given as 70. These men carried out their work of translation in separate rooms and produced results which were all exactly alike! It is most likely, however, that the Septuagint came into existence as a Greek Targum[1] just as in Palestine there came into existence an Aramaic Targum[1] for the help of those who were unable to understand the Hebrew Scriptures. The influence of the Septuagint upon the Jews of the Dispersion and even more upon the young Christian Church cannot be over-estimated. Apart from certain Greek overtones noticeable here and there which would remind its readers of its cultural background, it was almost negligible as a vehicle of Hellenization. But as an instrument for the propagation of Judaism throughout the Dispersion its contribution was of inestimable importance.

In Alexandria, too, many Gentile books were written and sent out to many parts of the world where, no doubt, they were studied by the more learned among the Jews. These often contained slanderous accusations against the Jewish race and religion which were commonly regarded as both superstitious and atheistic. The Jews, on their part, did not attempt to disguise, in their own writings, the utter contempt which they had for the heathen. Indeed the whole Jewish-Hellenistic literature, from the time of the Septuagint down to Josephus at the end of the first century A.D., had as its aim the condemnation of idolatry, chiefly by ridicule, and the defence of Judaism against the encroachments

---

[1] The word 'Targum' signifies a translation or paraphrase of the Hebrew Scriptures into the language of the people. In Aramaic-speaking lands the reading of the Scriptures in the synagogue was accompanied by an oral rendering (see pp. 63ff). This custom was believed to go back to the time of Ezra (cf. Neh. 8.8). By the second century A.D. Aramaic Targums were in existence in written form.

of such heathen influence.[1] Much of this literature is known to us only in fragments or in references in other works,[2] but those writings which have survived show quite clearly the mixture of Greek and Jewish thought that had taken place long before the beginning of the Christian era.

This is well illustrated in such books as the Sibylline Oracles (Book III) and the Wisdom of Solomon. These Sibylline Oracles were written during the latter half of the second century B.C. in Alexandria. They are imitative of the Greek 'Sibyls' which exercised a considerable influence on pagan thought both before and after this time. The pagan Sibyl was a prophetess who, under the inspiration of the god, was able to impart wisdom to men and to reveal to them the divine will. There were many varieties of such oracles in different countries, and in Egypt in particular they came to have an increasing interest and significance. The Alexandrian Jews saw in this type of literature an excellent medium of propaganda. By judicious alteration and expansion they used the framework of the pagan oracles to propagate the faith of 'the only true and living God'.

Of much greater significance is the Wisdom of Solomon, written in the first century B.C. by a Jew of Alexandria who, in presenting his faith, shows that he had been deeply influenced in his thinking by the outlook and philosophy of the Gentile Greek world and that he was no doubt well read in that field. This influence is seen, for example, in his treatment of the idea of 'wisdom' which he personifies in a way similar to the Stoic teaching concerning the all-pervading *Logos* or Word.[3] Here, indeed, is a bold attempt to bring together the piety of orthodox

[1] This was also the theme of other Jewish books, originating in Palestine, which in due course were translated into Greek and eventually found their way into the Septuagint, such as I Maccabees, Bel and the Dragon, Judith, the Rest of Esther, Tobit and Susanna (see pp. 78ff).

[2] See R. H. Pfeiffer, *History of New Testament Times, with an Introduction to the Apocrypha*, 1949, pp. 200ff.

[3] For a somewhat fuller treatment see pp. 23f.

Judaism and the Greek thought-forms of the age. In keeping with other Jewish writings of this time it incorporates a powerful polemic against the Gentiles and upholds as the true religion that revealed through God's servant Moses.

An outstanding example of Hellenistic Judaism is to be found in the Alexandrian Jewish writer Philo who was a contemporary of Jesus and of Paul. He was well read not only in the Hebrew Scriptures but in the Jewish Hellenistic writings and in the Greek philosophies as well. The aim of his writings was to demonstrate the relation between the religion of the Scriptures and the truth of the Greek philosophies. He made free use of the common Alexandrian practice of allegorism and by this means demonstrated, for example, that Moses was at one with the Greek philosophers. His position was not accepted by the orthodox Judaism of his day, but his approach to religion and philosophy and the relation between them had a very considerable influence on the development of Christian theology in the years to come.

c. *Greek culture in Palestine*

The impact of Hellenism on Judaism was felt even in Palestine itself where, for the most part, the Jews belonged to the Dispersion and lived as members of a Greek community. During the time of the Seleucids many cities in Palestine were won over to the Greek way of life and some new cities, modelled on Greek lines, came into being. These communities and their method of government by democratic senate resembling the Athenian *Boulē* or Council, elected annually and comprising representatives of the people, would bring to the Jews an entirely new mental outlook and a hitherto unknown insight into the Hellenistic culture and civilization much of which, to the loyal Jew, would appear to be unedifying and even subversive of the faith of Israel. Even in Jerusalem and its immediate environs there were many who adopted the Greek way of life as early as the period of Ptolemaic supremacy, and many more succumbed under the concentrated propaganda of the Seleucids. The First Book of Maccabees throws light on the situation at that time in these words, 'In those days there came forth out of Israel transgressors of the law, and persuaded many, saying, Let us go and make a covenant with the Gentiles that are around us; for since we parted from them many evils have befallen us. And the saying was good in their eyes. And certain of the people were forward herein, and went to the king, and he gave them licence to do after the ordinances of the Gentiles. And they built a place of exercise in Jerusalem according to the laws of the Gentiles; and they made themselves uncircumcised, and forsook the holy covenant, and joined themselves to the Gentiles, and sold themselves to do evil' (I Macc. 1.11-15). Commenting on this passage A. C. Purdy writes, 'Reading between the lines we may infer that the challenge to Judaism here was not that of a rival religion but of a rival culture. It was the challenge of secularism. The religion of the Jews was yet to be directly attacked, but a definite and aggressive Hellenism had appeared among them.'[1]

An important factor in spreading this 'rival culture' was undoubtedly the formation of gymnasiums which sprang up not only in Jerusalem but in many parts of the Dispersion, in Palestine and far beyond. 'They expressed,' writes Dr Edwin Bevan, 'fundamental tendencies of the Greek mind—its craving for harmonious beauty of form, its delight in the body, its unabashed frankness with regard to everything natural.'[2] The Greek emphasis on beauty, shape and movement would open up aesthetic horizons hitherto unknown to many Jews. For this reason some of the Jewish religious rites which appeared unaesthetic to the Greeks would be neglected by certain Jews. As the above quotation from I Maccabees shows, Jewish athletes, for example, who would

[1] G. H. C. Macgregor and A. C. Purdy, *Jew and Greek*, 1937, p. 30.
[2] *Jerusalem under the High Priests*, 1920, p. 35.

normally run naked on the track, became 'uncircumcised' by means of a slight surgical operation so as to avoid the derision of the crowd.

Games and races in the stadium and hippodrome were distinctive marks of the Hellenized city and were popular with Jewish youths no less than with those of other religious and cultural backgrounds. The theatre, too, played an important part in the dissemination of Greek culture. We know of Jews who themselves wrote tragedies in Greek verse and whose plays, like *The Exodus* by a certain Ezekiel, were no doubt performed in the theatre which Herod built near to the Temple in Jerusalem. Religious rites and ceremonies, with which many of the games and performances were associated, would have an inevitable influence on the Jewish population and would tend to corrupt the minds of the youth, accompanied as they often were by a measure of immorality and vice. For the Hellenism with which the Jews came into contact during this period, whilst containing much that was good and beautiful, had in the popular mind a close connection with 'the groves of Daphne, and the ways of soldiers, brothel-keepers and traders'.[1]

D. *The religious influence of Hellenism*

It is obvious from what has been said that the influence of Hellenism could not be confined to the strictly social or literary or cultural or aesthetic fields; by its very nature it created a definitely spiritual atmosphere which was in many respects completely foreign to the Jewish religious outlook. The various festivals and ceremonies, associated with almost every part of Greek social life, would leave their imprint on the religious life and customs of the people.

It is important in this connection to observe that Hellenism was a syncretistic system beneath whose surface the thought and

[1] G. H. C. Macgregor and A. C. Purdy, *op. cit.*, p. 143.

beliefs of many old eastern religions continued to exercise a potent influence. Within the Syrian branch of Hellenism, for example, the Zoroastrian religion of the old Persian Empire was very much alive.[1] In its earlier form at any rate Zoroastrianism taught a dualism in which there was envisaged an age-long struggle between the powers of light led by the good spirit Ahura-Mazda, and the powers of darkness led by the evil spirit Angra-Mainyu. This dualistic principle is worked out in a doctrine of 'the two ages' in which 'the present age' of ungodliness is set over against 'the future age' of righteousness. At last, through the good offices of Shaoshyant the saviour, Ahura-Mazda casts Angra-Mainyu into the abyss. The end of the world comes; the dead are raised and face the judgment. All men are subjected to the flame of a purifying fire; at last all are saved and the new age appears with a new heaven and a new earth.

Alongside the teaching of Zoroastrianism went the old Babylonian worship of the heavenly luminaries and especially the seven planets which, in their revolutions round the earth, were believed to control the lives of men and nations. The survival of this worship is quite understandable because the Persian Empire, which Alexander the Great had taken over, had itself succeeded the old Babylonian Empire and in the process had incorporated many of its customs and beliefs and had adopted its language, Aramaic or 'Chaldee', as the official language of government. There thus emerged a Perso-Babylonian syncretism, or 'mixture' of culture, which in course of time coloured deeply Syrian Hellenism.

Through the medium of Syrian Hellenism the impact of this culture would be felt by the Jews in Palestine. Indeed many of the Jews would have direct contact with Perso-Babylonian thought and culture because, from the time of the Captivity, they had lived side by side with Iranians (or Persians) in Mesopotamia.

[1] See pp. 95, 107ff, 112, 135.

From time to time those Babylonian Jews would return to Palestine, bringing back with them a sympathetic appreciation of some aspects of Persian thought, particularly those which were not necessarily incompatible with their own Hebrew religion. No doubt many would be attracted back to Palestine in the time of the Maccabees and their successors when a strong Jewish state came into being.

The influence of Zoroastrianism, and indeed of the whole Perso-Babylonian culture,[1] is amply illustrated in the writings of the Jewish apocalyptists of this period and even, though to a lesser extent, in the works of Pharisaic Judaism.[2] It is evident, too, in the writings of the Qumran Covenanters where there appears, for example, a form of dualism in many ways similar to that of Zoroastrianism which cannot be explained simply by reference to Old Testament religion.[3] An acquaintance with Zoroastrian eschatology (i.e. doctrine of 'the last things') is indicated in the Old Testament itself;[4] but the Jewish apocalyptists, including the writer of the Book of Daniel, are much more strongly influenced by it. Their whole outlook is governed by the belief that this present evil age was fast drawing to a close and that the new age would speedily be ushered in.[5] This dualistic view of the universe coloured their beliefs concerning the messianic hope, for example, which in course of time assumed transcendent characteristics[6] and also their conception of the life after death.[7] In this latter case Zoroastrian influence is evident in such matters as the separation of the soul from the body at death, the lot of the departed between death and resurrection, the doctrine of resurrection and their teaching concerning the Last

[1] Compare the interest shown in the heavenly bodies by such writings as Jubilees and I Enoch 72-82.
[2] See p. 50.
[3] Compare particularly the scroll entitled 'The War of the Sons of Light and the Sons of Darkness'.
[4] E.g. Isa. 24-27; 65.17ff.   [5] See pp. 94, 107ff, 120ff.
[6] See pp. 130ff.   [7] See chapter 7.

Judgment. Another realm in which this influence was deeply felt is in the greatly developed doctrine of angels and demons and in particular the personalization of evil spirits for which there is no parallel in the thought of the Old Testament.[1]

Even more important than Syrian Hellenism was Egyptian Hellenism which took shape under the Ptolemies. The old religious and mystical traditions of Egypt and Babylonia came into contact with the new Greek science and culture, producing a system of thought much more abstract in form than the Syrian branch of Hellenism. Many Jews, especially those of the Dispersion, were greatly influenced by the philosophical type of religion which accompanied this particular form of Greek culture.

This point is well illustrated by the author of the Wisdom of Solomon[2] whose familiarity with Greek thought is evident, for example, in his teaching concerning 'wisdom'. The idea of 'wisdom' is familiar enough to the reader of the Old Testament in such books as Proverbs, Job and Ecclesiastes, but in the Wisdom of Solomon the influence of Greek philosophy is most clearly marked. 'The author's teaching of divine and human wisdom', writes B. M. Metzger, '. . . is an explication of the earlier ideas on this subject expressed in the Book of Proverbs, with a metaphysical twist borrowed from the Stoic conception of the universal Logos, that impersonal mediator between God and creation.'[3] Having 'created the world out of formless matter' (11.17, cf. Gen. 1.2), God sends into this creation a soul which, to the writer of this book, is none other than wisdom itself. The spirit of wisdom comes from God (7.7, etc.) and is 'a clear effluence of the glory of the Almighty' (7.25). God created all things by his word (9.1), but wisdom was present before creation (9.9).

[1] See pp. 50, 112.
[2] See also IV Maccabees which shows an intimate knowledge of Greek philosophy, especially 1.13—3.18, 5.22-26, 7.17-23.
[3] *An Introduction to the Apocrypha*, 1957, p. 73.

Since then it has been 'the artificer' (7.22), the renewer (7.27), the orderer (8.1) and the performer (8.5) of all things. In 7.22f an attempt is made to define wisdom and no fewer than 21 qualities are ascribed to it; but even then it remains an enigma.

The influence of Greek thought on the Wisdom of Solomon is evident also in its teaching concerning the Platonic doctrine of the pre-existence of the soul, as in 8.19-20 where we read, 'Now I was a goodly child, and a good soul fell to my lot; nay rather, being good, I came into a body undefiled.'[1] This same idea is present in the Jewish writer Philo (died c. A.D. 50) and in such a book as II Enoch (A.D. 1-50) where these words appear: 'Sit and write all the souls of mankind, however many of them are born, and the places prepared for them to eternity; for all souls are prepared to eternity, before the foundation of the world' (23.4-5).

In most of those Jewish books (particularly those of an apocalyptic character) the belief is expressed in a resurrection from the dead in which the soul or spirit is re-united with the body,[2] but in a few of them the influence of Platonic thought is again evident in passages expressing belief in the immortality of the soul. In the Wisdom of Solomon 3.1-5, for example, we read, 'The souls of the righteous are in the hand of God, and no torment shall touch them. In the eyes of the foolish they seemed to have died; and their departure was accounted to be their hurt, and their journeying away from us to be their ruin; but they are in peace. For even if in the sight of men they be punished, their hope is full of immortality; and having borne a little chastening, they shall receive great good; because God made trial of them, and found them worthy of himself.' At least two other books express this same belief. In I Enoch 91-104 (c. 164 B.C.) the writer refutes the Sadducean view that there is no difference between the lot of the righteous and the lot of the wicked beyond death (102.6-8,

---

[1] Cf. also 15.8, 11; IV Macc. 13.13, 21; 18.23.   [2] See pp. 84, 146ff.

11) and affirms on the contrary that 'all goodness and joy and glory are prepared' for the souls of the righteous (103.3). They shall live and rejoice and their spirits shall not perish (103.4). So also in the Book of Jubilees (c. 150 B.C.) the righteous pass at once after death into the blessedness of immortality—'Their bones shall rest in the earth, and their spirits shall have much joy' (23.31).

The influence of these different types of Hellenism upon Judaism during this period is clear; but in its fundamental tenets Judaism remained true to the faith of its fathers and prepared the way not only for its own survival but also for the birth of the Christian religion.

2. THE REACTION AGAINST HELLENISM

Mention has been made of the policy of toleration followed by both Ptolemies and Seleucids by which Judaism and Hellenism were allowed to exist side by side. These were years of great peril for the Jewish faith. For this policy aimed at Hellenization through a gradual infiltration of Greek influence and a gradual assimilation to the Greek way of life. It was when this policy of peaceful penetration was replaced by a policy of persecution, notably in the reign of Antiochus IV (175-163 B.C.), that a violent reaction set in which developed in time into a burning hatred of the whole Hellenistic way of life.

A. *The Hellenizing party in Jerusalem*

Long before the reign of Antiochus IV there had been a strong Hellenizing party among the Jews in Palestine whose ringleaders were to be found chiefly in the ranks of the wealthy and priestly aristocracy who, by reason of their social position, enjoyed the privileges of the royal court and curried the favour of the king.

Moreover, this whole period was marked by bitter rivalry

between two great houses, the House of Tobias and the House of
Onias, each of which was to influence deeply the course of events
in the coming years, particularly in relation to the High Priestly
office. Josephus tells how the High Priest Onias II, 'a great lover
of money', refused to pay the annual tribute tax of 20 talents to
Ptolemy IV (221-203 B.C.), whereupon Joseph, son of Tobias,
had himself appointed tax collector for the whole country.
Joseph and his house became extremely rich and gained for
themselves a position of considerable power in the nation. And
so at this time the two rival houses were represented in the two
highest officers in the State.

In the time of Antiochus the Great (223-187 B.C.) the control of
Palestine passed over from the Ptolemies to the Seleucids and
forthwith Joseph and his followers transferred their allegiance to
that monarch whose government was direly in need of money.
There were men in Jerusalem who were ready to raise or offer
money in return for positions of power. Such a one was Simon
of the House of Tobias who, in the reign of Seleucus IV (187-175
B.C.), encouraged the king's chief minister to seize the sacred
moneys in the Temple and then tried to incriminate the High
Priest, Onias III. Riots broke out in Jerusalem and Onias III
set off for the Seleucid court to ask help from the king in quelling
the disturbances.

The feud between the two rival houses came to a head in the
reign of Antiochus IV (175-163 B.C.) who succeeded his brother
Seleucus. The Hellenizers in Jerusalem, and in particular the
aristocratic party who were openly pro-Syrian, saw in the accession of Antiochus an opportunity for gaining their ends. The
legitimate High Priest, Onias III, whose loyalties were pro-
Egyptian, was an obstacle to their hopes and so, during his
temporary absence from the country, and with the concurrence
of the king's government, his brother Jesus or Joshua (who
changed his name to the Greek form Jason) was appointed High

Priest in his stead with the help of a substantial bribe to the king (II Macc. 4.7-10). Antiochus no doubt regarded his appointment as a wise political move. Permission was given to re-model Jerusalem on Hellenistic lines (I Macc. 1.11-15); a gymnasium was built in Jerusalem and many Jews dressed after the Greek fashion.

The orthodox Jews, and in particular the Hasidim or Pious Ones (predecessors of the Pharisees),[1] were deeply incensed at these happenings and indeed at the spread of Hellenistic influence generally. To them the appointment of a High Priest was an act of God which had nothing to do with the approval or disapproval of a Gentile king. Their only consolation was that the new High Priest, Jason, was at least a member of the orthodox party. But this situation was soon to be altered, for at this point one Menelaus who was not even a member of the High Priestly family, ousted Jason from office with the help of the Tobiads and by offering to the king a larger bribe than his rival had given (II Macc. 4.23ff)! The followers of Menelaus openly supported the Greek way of life and set themselves up against the orthodox party. The split between the two sections of the people widened and fighting broke out in Jerusalem between the Hellenistic and the orthodox parties. Encouraged by a rumour that Antiochus had died in a campaign in Egypt (170-169 B.C.), Jason hurried to Jerusalem and drove out Menelaus (II Macc. 5.5ff).

The pattern was already set for the coming struggle. The conflict that was to follow was not simply a matter of 'Jews versus Syrians', but 'Jews versus Jews'; for, over against the Hellenizing party in Jerusalem, the vast majority of the Jews in the surrounding country were lined up in opposition to any policy of Hellenization. As Dr Oesterley remarks, 'During a considerable part of the second century B.C. "Jerusalem versus Judaea" correctly describes Jewish internal affairs.'[2]

[1] See pp. 49, 54f.   [2] *A History of Israel*, vol. 2, 1934, p. 259.

B. *The vengeance of Antiochus*

The rumour concerning the death of Antiochus was proved false and the king returned determined that Palestine must submit to his avowed policy of unifying his kingdom by means of Hellenic culture and religion. No doubt his determination was strengthened by reason of his fear of the growing power of Rome and of the consequent need to consolidate his Empire. The removal of his protégé Menelaus from the High Priestly office would be considered an affront to his royal dignity, and so he resolved to wreak vengeance on the Jews. Accordingly he attacked Jerusalem, drove out Jason and restored Menelaus to office. His soldiers were let loose and massacred many among the people; the Temple was desecrated and the sacred vessels plundered (I Macc. 1.20-28).

It soon became obvious that, although he had the support of the Hellenizers in Jerusalem, his policy of Hellenization was violently opposed by the bulk of the people who, in addition, refused to acknowledge Menelaus as High Priest. Accordingly Antiochus determined to wipe out the Jewish religion altogether (168 B.C.). He set about destroying those very features of Judaism which, ever since the time of the Captivity, had been regarded as distinctive characteristics of the Jewish faith (cf. I Macc. 1.41ff). All Jewish sacrifices were forbidden; the rite of circumcision was to cease; the Sabbath and feast days were no longer to be observed. Disobedience in any of these respects carried the penalty of death. Moreover, books of the Torah (or Law) were disfigured or destroyed; Jews were forced to eat swine's flesh and to sacrifice at idolatrous altars set up throughout the land. Then to crown his deeds of infamy he erected an altar to the Olympian Zeus, with an image of the god probably bearing the features of Antiochus himself, on the altar of burnt offerings within the Temple court (I Macc. 1.54). It is this altar which the writer of the Book of Daniel calls 'the abomination that desolates' (Dan. 11.31).

These events were followed by severe persecution in which many were put to death (I Macc. 1.57-64). To this period belong the stories, partly legendary, told in II Maccabees 6-7 of the martyrdom of Eleazar and the Seven Brothers. Many left the cities and crowded out into the villages where they were pursued by government agents intent on stamping out the Jewish faith.

c. *The Maccabees and the Maccabean Revolt*

Very soon passive resistance gave way to open aggression. The spark of revolt came from the village of Modein, north-west of Jerusalem, where a priest named Mattathias, of the House of Hasmon, lived with his five sons (I Macc. 2.1ff). When a Syrian official came to Modein to enforce heathen sacrifice, Mattathias not only refused to comply but slew a renegade Jew who did sacrifice and at the same time killed the Syrian official. This was the signal for Mattathias and his sons to flee to the mountains where they were joined by many zealous Jews (I Macc. 2.23-28). Of particular importance was the accession to their ranks of the Hasidim (I Macc. 2.42ff) to whom the whole Hellenistic culture and foreign influence were *anathema*, for their presence 'gave full religious sanction to the revolt'.[1] They can hardly be called a party within Judaism, but formed a very powerful body of opinion. They came in the main from the poorer classes and from the country districts but numbered among them some prominent men. Their obvious piety and religious zeal were to be vital factors in the future life of the nation. Their attitude is vividly expressed in the Book of Daniel which, in its present form at any rate, was composed in the time of Antiochus by one of the Hasidim.

The Revolt which followed was led in turn by three of

[1] H. Wheeler Robinson, *The History of Israel*, 1938, p. 176.

Mattathias's sons, Judas (166-160 B.C.) surnamed Maccabaeus ('the Hammerer' ?),[1] Jonathan (160-143 B.C.) and Simon (142-134 B.C.). Marked success followed their campaigns. On the 25th of Chislev (December), 165 B.C., on the very day on which it had been desecrated three years before (I Macc. 4.54), the Temple was cleansed and re-dedicated, under the leadership of Judas, and the worship restored (I Macc. 4.36ff; cf. II Macc. 10.1-7). This event has been commemorated ever since in the Jewish Festival of *Hanukkah* (Dedication), sometimes known as the Festival of Lights.[2] Fighting continued, but in 162 B.C. Lysias, regent of Antiochus V, made generous terms with Judas and granted a free pardon to the rebels and full religious liberty (I Macc. 6.58ff; cf. II Macc. 13.23f). To conciliate them further he commanded that Menelaus be put to death. The Hasidim, whose purpose had been religious and not political, by this time saw their aims fulfilled and so withdrew their support from the Maccabees. This is indicated in the support they gave to one, Alkimus, whom Demetrius I (successor to Antiochus V) appointed High Priest. He was recognized by the Hasidim as a true High Priest of the Aaronite line. Judas, however, was not content with religious freedom but sought political independence. After some initial success the Jews were defeated, however, and Judas himself was slain at Elasa in 160 B.C. (I Macc. 9.18f). Alkimus died shortly afterwards, and for the next seven years Jerusalem was without a High Priest.

Jonathan now succeeded his brother Judas as leader of the nationalist Jews with the help of his other brother Simon. It was a time of intrigue in which several rivals staked their claims to the Syrian throne. In 153 B.C. Demetrius I (162-150 B.C.) had to deal with such a rival in the person of Alexander Balas who claimed

[1] Strictly speaking the name 'Maccabean' should be applied only to Judas but is generally used with reference to his brothers also.
[2] Cf. John 10.22 where reference is made to it as 'the Feast of Dedication'.

to be the son of Antiochus IV. Both men tried to court the friendship of Jonathan, and in the end Balas (150-145 B.C.) outbid Demetrius by appointing him High Priest in 152 B.C. (I Macc. 10.15-17). It is to be observed that the orthodox party did not elect him High Priest but, at most, simply accepted the appointment made by the king. Jonathan was later confirmed in the High Priesthood by Tryphon who was acting on behalf of the infant son of Alexander Balas. But Tryphon, growing suspicious of Jonathan's power, killed him in 143 B.C. (I Macc. 12.48; 13.23).

Simon, who succeeded his brother Jonathan, set about consolidating his position. In 142 B.C. he won from Demetrius II (145-138 B.C.) immunity from taxes and the Jews proclaimed their independence (I Macc. 13.41). In 141 B.C. a further step was taken. A decree in bronze was set up in the Temple conferring on him the office of High Priest with hereditary rights: 'The Jews and the priests were well pleased that Simon should be their leader and high priest for ever, until there should arise a faithful prophet ... and Simon accepted hereof, and consented to be high priest, and to be captain and ethnarch of the Jews' (I Macc. 14.41, 47). The High Priesthood which had been hereditary in the House of Onias and had been usurped since the deposition of Onias III was now made hereditary in the Hasmonean[1] line. Here, then, we see the emergence of an independent Jewish state in which the civil head and the military leader were at the same time the High Priest. This union was to continue throughout the life of the Hasmonean House.[2] Simon, however, was not to be allowed to die in peace. In 134 B.C. he was treacherously slain by his son-in-law Ptolemy. His son, John Hyrcanus, now succeeded to the High Priesthood (I Macc. 16.13-17).

The Maccabees, in the name of Judaism, had won a resounding

[1] For the significance of this name see the following section.
[2] For the bearing of these events on the messianic hope see pp. 123f.

victory not only over their foreign enemies, but also over that whole culture which these enemies were determined to enforce upon them. But it would be false to imagine that the decisive victory had been won.

D. *The Hasmonean House*

The word 'Hasmonean' is derived from the family name of Mattathias and his sons who belonged to the House of Hasmon. It is by this name that the Maccabees are known in later Jewish literature, but it is convenient to reserve the expression 'Maccabee' for Judas and his two brothers and to use the title 'Hasmonean' to describe their descendants, five in number, under whom the Jews experienced almost seventy years of independence (134-63 B.C.). For a short time during the reign of John Hyrcanus (i.e. Hyrcanus I, 134-104 B.C.) Judaea became a vassal state, but independence was regained in 129 B.C. and was confirmed by the Roman Senate. Hyrcanus forthwith began to extend his territory. In the south, for example, he seized Idumaea, compelling the inhabitants to be circumcised; in the north he seized Samaritan territory, destroying the rival Temple on Mount Gerizim.[1]

These acts on the part of Hyrcanus show that he had obvious religious ideals, but during this whole period there was a growing discontent, chiefly on the part of the Hasidim and the orthodox Jews generally, with the Maccabees and the Hasmonean House. Not only had they taken over the High Priesthood, they had become increasingly worldly and irreligious. By the time of John Hyrcanus the growing breach within Judaism had materialized into two parties whose names now emerge for the first time as Pharisees and Sadducees.[2] At first Hyrcanus sided with the Pharisees, but when one of their number demanded that he should

[1] This Temple had been built probably some time in the fourth century.
[2] See pp. 49ff.

relinquish the High Priestly office he broke with them and joined forces with the party of the Sadducees.

Dr Oesterley points out[1] that one of the chief reasons why the Pharisees opposed the Hasmoneans was that they spoke of themselves as kings, although they were not of the lineage of David, and he indicates that even Hyrcanus assumed this royal office. Whether this was so or not, Josephus gives the information[2] that his successor, Aristobulus I (103 B.C.), was first to take the title of king, although this is not indicated on his coins. This fact, together with his support of the Sadducean party, his love of Greek culture and the fact that he was implicated in the murder of his mother and his brother Antigonus, roused the antagonism of the Pharisees still more.

Matters, however, came to a head in the time of his successor, Alexander Jannaeus (102-76 B.C.). At the very outset he greatly angered the Pharisees by marrying the widow of his brother Aristobulus, although it was unlawful for a High Priest to do this. Moreover, he neglected his spiritual office and devoted himself as a warrior to conquest and to aggrandizement by means of war. He used the title 'king', announcing the fact on his coins in Greek as well as in Hebrew characters, thus revealing his attachment to the Greek way of life and demonstrating a further stage in the secularization of the High Priesthood. His unpopularity with the people is illustrated by an incident which took place on one occasion at the Feast of Tabernacles. With complete unconcern for the responsibilities of his High Priestly office he purposely flouted ritual requirements by pouring out the water libation on the ground and not on the altar. So incensed were the people that they pelted him with the citrons which they had brought with them for use in the ritual. In a fit of temper he gave orders to his soldiers who slew many of the Jews within the courts of the

[1] *Op. cit.*, pp. 285f.   [2] *Antiquities* 13. 301; *Bellum Judaicum* 1. 70.

Temple. At a later date the situation became so bad that civil war broke out which lasted for six years. When at last peace was restored it is reported that he caused 800 Jews who had opposed him to be crucified.

During the rest of his reign the Pharisees and the orthodox remained quiet. But so powerful was the Pharisaic party becoming that Jannaeus, near the end of his life, saw in it a grave danger to the royal house. He accordingly advised his wife Alexandra, who was appointed queen by his command, to conciliate them by giving them more authority in the state. When Alexandra (75-67 B.C.) came to the throne on her husband's death she acted accordingly and appointed her elder son, Hyrcanus II, to be High Priest. Hyrcanus was favourably disposed towards the Pharisees and by his influence they grew considerably in strength. With increased civil and religious power in their hands they were able to impose their own views on the people. In particular they made matters very difficult for their Sadducean opponents who found a champion in Alexandra's younger son, Aristobulus, who made it clear that he was intent upon gaining the throne. On his mother's death Aristobulus gathered an army and defeated his brother near Jericho. Hyrcanus was forced to give up office and Aristobulus (66-63 B.C.) became king and High Priest, remaining in power until 63 B.C.

The story of the Hasmoneans draws to an end with the account of one Antipater, governor of Idumaea, who encouraged Hyrcanus in exile to remove his brother from office. With the help of an Arabian ruler, Aretas III, he besieged Aristobulus in Jerusalem. It was at this point that Rome decided to interfere in Palestinian affairs. Pompey sent his general, Scaurus, to quell the rising and he, through bribery, supported Aristobulus. In the year 63 B.C. Pompey in person, fearing the designs of Aristobulus, attacked Jerusalem and conquered it, entering in person into the Temple and the Holy of Holies. Aristobulus was carried captive to Rome.

Hyrcanus was confirmed in the High Priesthood and was appointed ethnarch of Judaea which was now added to the province of Syria.

E. *Herod and the Romans*

In 63 B.C., then, the Jews lost their independence when Pompey once again brought them 'under the yoke of the heathen'. From that time forward the spirit of Jewish nationalism sprang into revolt and continued right down to the destruction of Jerusalem and the Jewish state in A.D. 70.

The years following 63 B.C. were very troubled ones indeed whose complications can only be lightly touched upon here. Antipater, whose name is prominent in Jewish history for the next twenty years, at first gave strong support to Pompey, but in 48 B.C. when Pompey was overthrown he transferred his support to his rival Caesar. As a result, Caesar granted very considerable privileges to the Jews, not only in Judaea but also in the Dispersion. Antipater he made governor of Judaea, conferring upon him Roman citizenship. But, despite all the benefits accruing from his friendship with Caesar, Antipater was bitterly hated by the Jews, no doubt because of his very dependence upon Rome and because of his Idumean (i.e. Edomite) birth. This hatred was intensified when, after the death of Caesar in 44 B.C., the proconsul Cassius came into Syria and, with the utmost severity, exacted heavy taxation from the people. The following year Antipater was poisoned by his enemies.

When Antony came to power after the battle of Philippi in 42 B.C. he made Antipater's two sons, Phasael and Herod, tetrarchs under the ethnarch Hyrcanus II whom he confirmed in the High Priesthood. But serious trouble lay ahead. Antigonus, son of Aristobulus the Hasmonean, gained the support of the Parthians who upheld his claims to the throne. Phasael and

Hyrcanus were taken prisoner; the former committed suicide and the latter was taken into exile. Herod, however, escaped and made straight for Rome where he secured an interview with Antony. There, much to his own surprise, he was appointed king of Judaea (40 B.C.). He had still, however, to face Antigonus who had taken possession of Judaea. With Roman help he defeated his rival in 37 B.C. after a three months' siege of Jerusalem. Antigonus was put to death and the reign of Herod the Great began.

Under Herod (37-4 B.C.) and his sons the policy of Hellenization went on apace. He wanted, if at all possible, to be 'everything to all men'—to the Jews a Jew, to the pagans a pagan. His marriage to Mariamne, the grand-daughter of Hyrcanus, was an indication of his desire to please the Jews as was, for example, his building of the new Temple at Jerusalem, begun in the year 20 B.C. But even this could not reconcile the people to his Idumean birth and to his plans to Hellenize the kingdom. In one important respect he alienated many of his Jewish subjects. In the Hasmonean dynasty the High Priest and the king were one. Now Herod, being an Idumean, could not be High Priest and so he made it his policy as much as possible to degrade that office. With this in view he broke the hereditary principle on which it had been based and abolished the life-long tenure of the office. Thereafter the High Priest was appointed by him and held office just as long as it pleased the king.

The policy of Hellenization on which Herod embarked was due, in part at least, to the very nature of his kingdom which contained many Greek cities and numbered many Greeks among its citizens. He has sometimes been called 'a patron of Hellenism', and this title can be fully justified in a number of respects. For example, he made little use of the Jewish Sanhedrin and in its place set up a royal council on Hellenistic lines; he replaced the old hereditary aristocracy by a new aristocracy of service and graded this new class according to Hellenistic practice. His policy of administration, of the nature of a strongly centralized bureaucracy, was pursued also along Hellenistic lines. The historian Josephus tells us that 'he appointed solemn games to be celebrated every fifth year in honour of Caesar, and built a theatre at Jerusalem, as also a very great amphitheatre in the plain' (*Ant.*, 15.8.1, sect. 267-69). He was a liberal supporter of the Olympic Games and 'was declared in the inscriptions of the people of Elis to be one of the perpetual managers of those games' (*Ant.*, 16.5.3, sect. 149). His extensive building operations support the contention that he encouraged the cult of the Emperor, for all the many temples he built throughout Palestine were dedicated to Caesar. The Pharisees in particular were horrified when they learned that Herod had actually permitted pagans in his kingdom to erect statues to himself. We read of certain men, worthy successors of the early Maccabees, who entered into a holy covenant to hinder him, even on pain of death, from perpetrating his policy of Hellenization. Even when they were captured and tortured and put to death there were others ready to take their place.

Following the death of Herod in 4 B.C. tumults broke out in Galilee which from this time forward was known as the hot-bed of Jewish nationalism. Josephus tells us of one Judas the Galilean who, in association with Zadduk the Pharisee, rebelled against Rome and founded a new sect in A.D. 6. This is presumably the party later to be known as the Zealots (in Greek) or Cananeans (in Aramaic) or Sicarii (in Latin) which was to be a thorn in the flesh of the Romans for many years to come. The rebellion in Galilee was put down with bloodshed by Herod's son Archelaus (4 B.C.-A.D. 6) who succeeded him as governor of Judaea only to be banished ten years later by the Romans as the result of an appeal against him by Jews and Samaritans. Apart from a short period of three years in which Herod's grandson, Agrippa I

(A.D. 41-44), ruled as king in Judaea, the country was governed by a succession of Roman procurators (A.D. 6-66). During the whole of this period Jewish nationalism was increasing in intensity and found a particularly dangerous expression in the activities of the Zealots who regarded the foreign rule of the Romans as an intolerable situation. These activities were motivated not simply by political aims but also by deep religious convictions, for it would seem that the Zealots regarded themselves as in the true line of succession of the early Maccabees.

It is interesting to recall that at least one of Jesus' disciples belonged, or had belonged, to this party. He is called Simon the Zealot (Luke 6.15, Acts 1.13) or Simon the Cananean (Matt. 10.4, Mark 3.18). It has been argued[1] that others may have belonged also, such as Judas Iscariot (from Latin *sicarius*, 'an assassin' ?), Simon Bar Jona (from Accadian *barjona*, 'a terrorist' ?) and James and John the 'sons of thunder' (Mark 3.17). On at least one occasion Paul was thought to be a Zealot (Acts 21.38) and Jesus himself was brought into association with leaders of the Zealot movement by the teacher Gamaliel (Acts 5.36, 37). Jesus was not a Zealot, but no doubt certain of his fellow-Jews and of the Romans thought of him as such.

The Zealots were essentially men who were zealous for God; they were the agents of his wrath against the idolatrous ways of the heathen. They believed that they were called by God to engage in a Holy War against 'the powers of darkness'. In this they shared the convictions of many other patriotic Jews including the Covenanters of Qumran.[2] Indeed in this respect, apart from the collaborationist Sadducees, there is at times no clear line of demarcation between one sect and another. Even Josephus, who is anxious to isolate the Zealots and to put on them alone the blame for the Jewish War, on at least one occasion links Zealots

---

[1] Cf. O. Cullmann, *The State in the New Testament*, 1956, pp. 15ff.
[2] See pp. 54ff.

and Essenes together and, as we have seen,[1] associates them in their origin with a Pharisee. Their patriotism was no doubt more obviously expressed than that of the others and their zeal for God made them only too ready to wield the sword as a divinely appointed instrument of salvation, but as Dr W. R. Farmer puts it, 'When the showdown came, the whole nation would be caught up in the life-and-death struggle between God's people and their enemies. Every patriotic Jew, whether he be Pharisee, Essene or Zealot, would be called upon to give his full measure of service in the Holy War.'[2] The same writer remarks that the Zealots were no doubt considered by many of their compatriots as 'over zealous' and 'a bit trigger-happy' in comparison with the other parties in the land. What is certain is that they did much to set off the war with Rome which raged from A.D. 66-70 and ended with the destruction of Jerusalem and the entire Jewish state. Only once more, in the year A.D. 132, was an attempt made to strike a blow for the independence of Judaism in a revolt led by one Ben Kosebah, commonly called Bar Kochba, and aided by the influential Rabbi Akiba. Three years later the rebellion was crushed and Jerusalem was refashioned as a Gentile city.

The struggle between Judaism and Hellenism was over and to all appearances the battle had been lost. But just as Hellenism could not be resisted by force alone, so Judaism could not be slain by power of arms. The Jewish state fell, but Judaism prevailed, for when conquest was denied and compromise forbidden, unlike Christianity which went out into the Hellenistic world to 'out-think and out-live and out-die' the pagans, it chose for itself the path of separation. This momentous step was taken by one Johanan ben Zakkai who, when the battle was raging for the life of Jerusalem just before its fall, set off for the town of Jamnia on the Palestinian coast and there founded a school which was to

[1] See p. 37.   [2] *Maccabees, Zealots and Josephus*, 1956, p. 183.

mark the beginning of a new era for the Jewish people. They no longer had Jerusalem; they no longer had the Temple; but there at Jamnia they had the study of the sacred Law of God, and that to them was more than life itself. For this their fathers had fought and died; for this their sons would live.

2

The People of the Book

THE struggle between Judaism and Hellenism described in the last chapter cannot be explained with reference to the desire of the Jews either for 'political freedom' or for 'religious liberty'. Indeed, the struggle went on even when 'political freedom' had been gained; and 'religious liberty', in the sense of each man's right to follow the dictates of his own conscience, would not have been tolerated by the Jews. 'Throughout this period', writes Dr T. W. Manson, 'the Jews were fighting, not for such modern ideals as these, but for the life of "Israel", where "Israel" is a complex organic whole which includes the monotheistic faith, the cultus in Temple and Synagogue, the law and custom embodied in the Torah, the political institutions which had grown up in the post-exilic period, the claim to ownership of the Holy Land, and whatever dreams there may have been of an Israelite world-rule to supersede the rule of the Gentile empires.'[1]

The new order of things contained in these ideals for which Judaism was willing to fight to the death had already found expression near the beginning of the third century B.C. in some words of the High Priest, Simon the Just. In the Jewish tractate Pirke Aboth 1.2 it is written, 'He used to say: on three things the world standeth: on the Torah, and on the (Temple) Service, and on the doing of kindnesses.' These three things represent

[1] T. W. Manson, *The Servant-Messiah*, 1956, p. 5.

41

'revelation, worship and sympathy, i.e. God's word to man, man's response to God, and man's love to his fellow men',[1] and are at one and the same time the rule of life and the foundation of the nation and state of Israel. In pre-Maccabean days the Temple still stood as a bulwark against the tide of Hellenism but, as we shall see, the rallying point for the forces of Judaism came more and more to be the eternal and sacred Torah.

I. TORAH RELIGION

Dr G. F. Moore defines the word 'Torah' as 'the comprehensive name for the divine revelation, written and oral, in which the Jews possessed the sole standard and norm of their religion'.[2] The word signifies 'instruction' or 'teaching' and indicates the revelation given by God to Israel through his servant Moses. The word is often translated 'Law', but this can be misleading, for its meaning is nearer to 'revelation' than it is to 'legislation'. But since this 'revelation' finds written expression in the Pentateuch, the name 'Torah' is commonly applied to the 'five books of Moses'. As we shall see, the name could be applied not only to the written record of this revelation but also to the unwritten tradition which sought to make explicit teaching which was implicit in the written Torah.

Throughout the whole of the period from Antiochus IV (175-163 B.C.) to Vespasian (A.D. 69-79) and Titus (A.D. 79-81) Jewish nationalism was rooted and grounded in the Torah. Within this word lay the germs of revolt which were to spell death to Hellenism and all that that foreign culture stood for within the Jewish nation. And so the Book, the vehicle and expression of Torah, became increasingly the sign and symbol of their faith.

[1] R. H. Charles, *Apocr. and Pseud.*, 1913, p. 691.
[2] *Judaism*, vol. 2, 1927, p. 263.

A. *From Temple to Torah*

Space does not permit to tell the story of Ezra who, according to the Talmud,[1] 'founded' the Torah long after it had been forgotten, and only brief mention can be made of the Sopherim or Scribes who, according to tradition, carried on the work of Ezra by teaching and interpreting the Torah to succeeding generations, claiming for it a position of supreme authority within Judaism. Their teaching was based on simple exegesis of the Torah out of which new traditions would arise for which there had been no precedent in the ancient store of tradition or in the Torah itself.[2]

The part played by the oral teaching of the Scribes was a very significant one and did much to prepare the people for the troublous years which were to follow in which the influence of Hellenistic culture began to make itself very deeply felt. There is reason to believe that the Sopherim organized weekly gatherings not only in Jerusalem but in the towns and villages round about at which the Torah was publicly read and explanations of it given. It would be a mistake to think of these gatherings in terms of the Synagogue services which subsequently grew up and spread rapidly throughout Jerusalem and the Dispersion, but they undoubtedly prepared the way for them, and to the Sopherim and their successors is due much of the credit for the development of this vitally important institution within Judaism.

On the death of Simon the Just about the year 270 B.C. the influence of the Sopherim came to an end, but there is evidence that after that date a body of men, chiefly lay, continued to apply themselves privately to a study of the Torah. This period of unauthoritative teaching continued till about 196 B.C., when it was probably brought to an end by the organization of what later

[1] See p. 68, n. 3.   [2] See further pp. 64ff.

came to be known as the Sanhedrin, a court with both priestly and lay members which applied itself to the regulation of religious affairs.

Thus, long before the time of the Maccabean Revolt, the common people had been grounded in the faith and had been taught to apply their religion to their everyday life in the new situation and conditions developing in Palestine. The Torah became increasingly the focus of their attention and gradually came to mean more and more in the devotional life of many who, by reason of the troubles of the times or by reason of their dispersion far from Jerusalem, were unable to offer sacrifices in the Holy Temple.

Somewhere, then, between the completion of the Torah about the middle of the fourth century B.C. and the Maccabean Revolt in 167 B.C. there took place a subtle transfer of emphasis from the Temple to the Torah which was yet to be of momentous importance for the life of Judaism. But it is in the Maccabean age that this transfer is most noticeable, for by then the Torah had become the visible symbol of the Jewish faith. The triumph of the Maccabean Revolt and the development of the Synagogue and the Schools both in Jerusalem and in the Dispersion would further enhance the reputation of the Torah. The Synagogue Torah was in no way opposed to the Temple ritual, but it fostered a deep personal religion—something which the Temple rites were unable to do. And so there came a time when the written record could take the place of the cultic acts in the affections of the people. This explains why, on the destruction of the Temple in A.D. 70, Judaism was yet able to survive. The ritual of the Temple had been replaced by reverence for the Torah; the priest had given way to the Rabbi; the Temple was supplemented by the Synagogue. Judaism thereafter was to be essentially a religion of the Book.

44

B. *The rallying point of revolt*

The centrality of the Torah for the movement of Jewish nationalism can be amply illustrated both from the Seleucid and from the Roman periods in each of which it became the rallying point of revolt. When Mattathias, for example, in the time of Antiochus IV defied the might of the Syrians at Modein, he cried aloud to the people, 'Whosoever is zealous for the Torah, and maintaineth the covenant, let him come forth after me' (I Macc. 2.27). It is surely very significant indeed that, despite the fact that the Temple had been desecrated only a short time before (I Macc. 1.54), it was not the Temple but the Torah to whose defence and support the people were summoned. An appeal to the Temple would have rallied a section of the people; but an appeal to the Torah had a greater chance of rallying the whole people; and, even if not all responded, all were involved, for the whole nation reverenced the Torah as the declared will and revelation of God. 'From first to last', writes Dr Travers Herford, 'the struggle was between Hellenism on the one side and the Torah on the other; and the final result was that Hellenism was routed and the Torah left supreme, more or less acknowledged by everyone and openly challenged by no one.'[1]

The enemies of the Jews were quick to recognize the reliance which they put on the Torah and the enthusiasm with which they rallied to its defence. And so the written Torah became the focus of their attack upon Judaism. Concerning the persecution of Antiochus IV, we read, 'And they rent in pieces the books of the Law which they found, and set them on fire. And wheresoever was found with any a book of the covenant, and if any consented to the law, the king's sentence delivered him unto death' (I Macc. 1.56, 57). To attack the Torah was to attack Judaism itself; to defend the Torah was to defend the faith of their fathers.

[1] *Talmud and Apocrypha*, 1933, p. 80.

The Maccabean Revolt began, continued and ended, then, in a summons to rise in defence of the Torah which was to the Jews the very embodiment of their religion. The challenge of Hellenism was not simply a matter of politics or aesthetics or morals or culture; it was a blow struck at the very roots of the Jewish faith which found expression in the sacred Torah, and so had to be resisted with all their powers.

But, as we have already seen, the Maccabean Revolt, though it won a great victory, did not settle the issue of 'Judaism versus Hellenism' once and for all. The Jewish nation was still surrounded by Hellenistic culture and had somehow to work out its relations to its environment. Throughout the time of the Hasmoneans in particular the development of the Synagogues and the Schools, in both of which teaching was given in the sacred Torah, helped greatly to counteract the infiltration of Hellenism into the life of the nation. But with the advent of Rome Hellenizing influences began again to assert themselves in more blatant forms and had to be resisted. The battle had to be fought all over again, and once more the Torah was to be the rallying point of revolt. Josephus, for example, writing of the Jews who opposed the Hellenizing policy of Herod, speaks of 'that undaunted constancy they showed in the defence of their laws' (*Ant.*, 15.8.4, sect. 291). These words may be taken as a true description of the attitude of the Jews to the Romans right through this period and up to the fall of Jerusalem in A.D. 70. Again and again Josephus tells how they were willing not only to fight and kill for the Torah, but to suffer and die for its sake.

As in the case of the Seleucids so also in the case of the Romans, the enemies of the Jews were quick to see where the centre of their loyalty lay, and so attack after attack was launched against the Torah. It is most significant that among the trophies from the Temple which Titus carried with him in triumphal procession in Rome was a copy of the Jewish Torah, and that behind it were carried images of *Nikē*, the Greek goddess of victory. The Torah is here regarded as the supreme symbol of Judaism over which the forces of enlightened Hellenism, it was believed, had prevailed.

c. *The Holy Covenant*

This zeal which the Jews showed for the Torah throughout the whole Hellenistic period was, however, not simply zeal for a Book, but rather for the Covenant to which the Book testified, a Covenant made by God in which he had set the Jewish nation apart to be his peculiar people. To despise the Torah was to betray the Covenant which God had made with their fathers. This helps to explain the fanatical loyalty which many Jews showed to the rites of their faith throughout those troublous days.

Circumcision, for example, was a visible sign that a man was a member of the Covenant (I Macc. 1.48, etc.), and so to submit to 'uncircumcision' was to deny that Covenant altogether (I Macc. 1.15). To eat swine's flesh was to do what the Torah forbade and so must be resisted on penalty of death (cf. I Macc. 1.62, 63; II Macc. 6.18, 7.1 for stories of outstanding heroism). The Sabbath was equally a mark of the Covenant which Hellenism sought to profane (II Macc. 6.6); so strictly did the Jews observe it that many of them chose death rather than lift up arms even to defend themselves on the Sabbath day (II Macc. 6.11; I Macc. 2.29-38). The Torah was uncompromising in its prohibition of idolatry in any shape or form; hence the bitter hatred of the Jews for anything that savoured of the cult of the Emperor; hence also their violent opposition to those buildings in the Greek style decorated with the idolatrous figures of animals and men; even the trophies which adorned the theatres were looked upon by many as images and so were *anathema* to the Jews who worshipped a 'jealous God' who would brook no rival to his throne.

The place which the Torah held, and still holds, in the life of Judaism is well summed up in these words of Dr H. Wheeler Robinson, 'The Law was the charter of Judaism, the real source of its strength through the many centuries. The institutions which it enjoined were, in large measure, brought to an end in A.D. 70; but the Law showed its power by the creation of a new Judaism, able to endure without land, city or temple. Through the reading of the Law, supplemented by that of the prophets, in the scattered synagogues of the Dispersion, the knowledge of the one holy God and of His covenant with Israel was kept fresh in the hearts of all.'[1]

2. THE TORAH AND THE SECTS

The Judaism of the period with which we are dealing was a most complex system, containing within itself many different parties and groups and sects whose names and distinctive beliefs have not always been recorded in history. Josephus states that 'the Jews had for a great while had three sects of philosophy' (a most misleading expression)—the Pharisees, the Sadducees and the Essenes to which he adds the party founded by Judas and Zadduk later to be given by him the name 'Zealots' (cf. Ant., 18.1.1-6, sect. 9-23). These were undoubtedly very influential parties within Judaism during this period, but to keep matters in proportion, we must remember that they were a very small minority in Palestine. It has been calculated that Pharisees, Sadducees and Essenes together would number only 30,000-35,000 out of a total of 500,000-600,000 in the time of Jesus. The Pharisees would number about five per cent of the total population and the Sadducees and Essenes together about two per cent.[2]

Some of the many groups in Judaism would have closer

---

[1] *Religious Ideas of the Old Testament*, 1913, p. 128.
[2] Cf. T. W. Manson, *op. cit.*, p. 11.

affinities with these three main sects than with others, but it is an oversimplification of the case to assume that, when these sects have been named, the only ones left over were the so-called '*Am ha-aretz* or 'people of the land'. Interesting light has been thrown on this situation by the discovery of the literature of the Qumran Covenanters near the shores of the Dead Sea. Attempts have been made to identify this community with one or other of the main sects and, whilst this is quite possible, the Qumran Sect could quite well represent an influential group within the nation in many respects different from those parties whose names are familiar to us. To quote the words of R. H. Pfeiffer, 'Judaism in the period under consideration was so alive, so progressive, so agitated by controversies, that under its spacious roof the most contrasting views could be held.'[1]

But all these groups or sects, it would seem, had one thing in common: they all owed allegiance to the Torah. It is quite wrong to single out, say, the Pharisees and name them 'the Torah party' or to ascribe to them willy-nilly writings of this period which exalt 'the Law of God'. The Torah was the very ground-work of Judaism and the foundation of their nationhood. This is not to say, however, that all the parties agreed on the significance of the Torah or on its interpretation. In point of fact there were greatly divergent opinions on this very matter so that, whereas their loyalty to the Torah was a bond of union, their conception of it was a constant cause of division among them.

A. *The Pharisees*

According to Josephus (*Ant.*, 13.5.9, sect. 171-3) the Pharisees existed in the time of Jonathan (160-143 B.C.), but elsewhere (*Ant.*, 13.10.5-7, sect. 288-99) he states that they first appear historically in conflict with John Hyrcanus[2] (134-104 B.C.). They exercised a great influence over a period of about three

[1] *Op. cit.*, p. 53.   [2] Or Jannaeus in the Talmud.

centuries and did more than any other party to determine the shape of Judaism in the years to come. Their spiritual ancestry is probably to be traced back to the Hasidim whose support of the Maccabees had given religious sanction to their bid for freedom. They were not a political party but essentially a religious sect, drawn largely from the middle class in society, which came increasingly to hold a strong religious and social position in the community.

Various explanations have been given of the name Pharisee such as 'expounder' (of scripture in the interests of the oral law) or 'separatist' (from unclean things or in the sense of 'expelled', viz. from the Sanhedrin). Dr T. W. Manson holds[1] that the word signifies 'Persian' and was applied to them by their opponents who in this way dubbed them as innovators in theology. Later on the name was given 'an edifying etymology' and was connected with the Hebrew root meaning 'to separate' and so came to be understood as 'separatist'. It is certainly true that, though the Pharisees were staunch supporters of 'tradition', to them it was no dead thing, and undoubtedly in certain of their doctrines (e.g. the Messianic Kingdom, the life beyond, belief in a multiplicity of demons and angels, etc.) they were influenced by Persian thought.

Throughout the whole of this period, however, they stood as a bulwark against the encroachments of Hellenism by showing themselves to be doughty champions of Torah religion. But it was in their interpretation of Torah that they differed most from their opponents, the Sadducees. The Pharisees maintained that the oral law should be regarded as of equal authority with the written Torah (cf. *Ant.*, 13.10.6, sect. 297), whereas the Sadducees upheld the sacred authority of the written Torah as completely above and apart from the new traditions and observances.[2]

[1] *Op. cit.*, pp. 19f.   [2] See chapter 3.

By teaching and interpreting the Torah, both written and oral, and by applying it to every-day life they 'democratized religion', making it personal and operative in the experience of the common people. Their chief instrument in propagating the Torah was the Synagogue, which became a most powerful institution within Judaism not only in Jerusalem, but also throughout the whole Dispersion. The reading of the Torah accompanied by an interpretative translation into the vernacular became a distinctive feature of the Synagogue service. In this the Scribes, many of whom were members of the Pharisaic party, would have an important rôle to play. The Gospels give some indication of the position which the Synagogues had come to hold as strongholds of Torah religion even before the time of Jesus.

But it is clear from the records that Pharisaism was at heart legalistic in character, and legalism can easily lead to formalism, and formalism to externalism and unreality, defects which revealed themselves in course of time in at least some phases of Pharisaism.[1] But, in spite of this, the Pharisees created a spirit of true piety and devotion which deeply affected the lives of the people and developed a religious individualism which gave a new relevance to the Torah of God.

B. *The Sadducees*

If the Pharisees as a whole belonged to the middle class, the Sadducees were represented by the wealthy aristocracy and particularly by the powerful priesthood in Jerusalem. Probably most of the Sadducees were priests, but they are not to be identified with the whole body of priesthood. They numbered in their ranks rich merchants, government officials and others. In origin, therefore, they were not a religious party, although that is what they tended to become; rather were they a body of people sharing

---

[1] Cf. Matt. 9.14; 15.10-20; 16.6; 23 *passim*; Mark 12.38-40; Luke 11.37-54; 16.14ff; 18.10ff; 20.46f, etc.

a common social standing and loosely bound together by a common determination to maintain the existing régime. Indeed, Dr T. W. Manson claims that the name originates in the Greek word *syndikoi* which in Athenian history signifies those who defend the existing laws against innovation.[1] Moreover, they adopted in religious matters a position of a distinctly conservative kind. The High Priest and his circle were members of the Sadducean party up to nearly A.D. 70, although some years before that time the Pharisees and latterly the Zealots had gained control of the Temple. Their influence had been determined by their position in the state, and when that was lost their influence ceased with it.

Like the Pharisees they believed in the supremacy of the Torah, but unlike them they refused to acknowledge the binding authority of the oral law. They had, it is true, traditions and usages of their own both ritual and legal, but as these did not trace their origin back to Moses they were not regarded as being on a level with the Torah. Moreover they believed that it was mainly in the Temple that the words of the Torah could be obeyed and that the ordinances provided by the priests on their own authority were a sufficient guide for the people in their fulfilment of it. In effect, whilst upholding the authority of the written Torah over against that of the oral tradition, the Sadducees regarded it as little more than a relic of the past.

If to the Pharisees the Torah was the centre of their faith, to the Sadducees it was the circumference within which could be entertained beliefs and practices foreign to Judaism. Hence their ability to take into their system many Hellenistic influences which were hateful to their fellow Jews.

c. *The Essenes*

The name Essene probably derives from an Aramaic word

[1] *Op cit.*, pp. 15f.

meaning 'holy' or 'pious' and corresponds to the Hebrew *hasid*. Relatively little is known about the Essenes, but the Roman historian Pliny tells of a people of this name, forming a closely knit community of an ascetic type, who lived near the western shore of the Dead Sea. Josephus and Philo give additional information that there were about 4,000 Essenes who, for the most part, lived in villages, although certain of them lived in the cities. These latter were no doubt regarded by their brethren as associate members of the community which lived in the wilderness under the strictest discipline. The name Essene probably covers a number of groups whose beliefs and practices, though perhaps not identical, were yet similar.

Of significance for our purpose is the recorded fact that this sect spent much time in the study and interpretation of the Torah and of other sacred books of which they took the greatest possible care. Josephus tells us of their intensive study of the Scriptures and indicates that certain of their number were able to foretell the future by their reading of the sacred books. Philo refers to their method of group study and states that one member of the group would read a passage aloud to the others and a more experienced brother would then explain the meaning of it. It is obvious that the written Torah and its study formed the basis of their communal life and was the inspiration of their movement. In their religious outlook they had much in common with the Pharisees, but in some respects at least appear to have been more strict than they in their interpretation of the Torah.

D. *The Zealots*

We have already observed that Josephus traces back the origin of the Zealots to the year A.D. 6; but in fact their roots go much further back into the pre-Roman period, for they may justifiably be regarded as true spiritual children of the Maccabees. Dr R. H.

Pfeiffer puts the position succinctly in these words, 'As the Pharisees are the heirs of the Hasidim, so the Zealots are the heirs of the Maccabees.'[1]

They are described by Josephus as brigands, robbers and the like, but they might equally well be described as patriots, according to the point of view of the writer; and Josephus was more than a little biased! It is wrong, however, to regard them simply as a radical political group within the state who stirred up trouble with the Romans. No doubt they attracted to themselves many of the riff-raff of their day with 'gangster' tendencies, but they were essentially a company of Jewish patriots motivated by deep religious convictions. It is of interest to note that Josephus describes the successive leaders of the Zealot movement by the word 'sophist' which may well indicate that within the party there was a planned programme of teaching going beyond the merely political interest which Josephus implies.

Indeed we know that their opposition to Rome was rooted in their zeal for the Torah. It was this zeal and not simply 'love of country' that engendered their patriotism and fanaticism, which came to be feared by friend as well as by foe. Josephus further tells us (*Ant.*, 18.1.6, sect. 23) that they had 'an inviolable attachment to liberty'; they refused to call any man 'lord' or to pay tribute to any king, for God was their only Ruler and Lord; they despised pain and made light of dying; even the suffering of relatives and friends would not move them from their purpose. Behind all this lay their passionate devotion to the Torah for which they were willing not only to fight but, when the call came, even to lay down their lives.

E. *The Covenanters of Qumran*

Mention has already been made of the Hasidim who, in the time of John Hyrcanus (134-104 B.C.), appeared as the party of

---

[1] *Op. cit.*, p. 36.

the Pharisees. Not all the Hasidim, however, identified themselves with this party. There seems reason to believe that, during the course of the second century B.C., a group of people in the true hasidic tradition elected to withdraw to the wilderness of Judaea under the leadership of one whom they called 'the Teacher of Righteousness' who formed his followers into a well-organized religious community, taught them a new interpretation of the Scriptures and bound them together by a 'new covenant' which pledged them to obedience to the Law of God until the dawning of the messianic age. The discovery in 1947 of these Covenanters' headquarters at Qumran near the shores of the Dead Sea and of a vast number of writings from their libraries has added much to our understanding of the state of affairs in Palestine during the inter-testamental period.

Ever since the finding of these 'Dead Sea Scrolls' opinion has been divided as to the identity of the Qumran community. Some scholars have argued for a pre-Maccabean date and others for an identification with the Zealots in the first century A.D. Perhaps the strongest arguments, however, can be brought forward for associating them, if not identifying them, with a branch of the Essenes from about the time of Alexander Jannaeus (102 B.C.) or a little earlier. At about the same period we have evidence of a large community of Essenes and an equally large community of Covenanters both living at or around the Wady Qumran, and the indication is that they were probably one and the same. This conviction is strengthened by a comparison of the customs, rites and beliefs of these two sects which indicate that they belonged to the same general type.

Of particular interest is the fact that both sects spent much time in the study and interpretation of the Torah and of the other sacred books. Among the Covenanters, whenever the full members of the Council met together in groups of ten, as was the custom, matters were so arranged that some member of the group was always engaged in study or exposition. Ordinary members of the Community were to devote the first third of every night to reading 'the Book', studying the law and responding with the appropriate blessings. Like the Essenes the Covenanters would have much in common with the Pharisees, but would be more strict than they in their interpretation of the Torah, as, for example, in their observance of the Sabbath day. They believed that their faithfulness as the representative remnant of Israel would bring about a vicarious expiation for their nation and would help to usher in the new age of which the prophets had spoken. This faithfulness was to find its expression in their meticulous study and practice of the Law, and it was for this purpose that they went out at the first into the wilderness of Judaea.

The leader of this community, the Teacher of Righteousness, taught his followers a new interpretation of the Scriptures which made clear to them the part they had to play in the fulfilment of God's purpose for their generation. Of particular significance were the writings of the prophets who, it was believed, wrote not simply of their own day but of the time of the end. In the prophecy of Habakkuk, the Covenanters saw a foretelling of the days in which they themselves were then living. The end was near at hand. The 'mystery' (Hebrew: *raz*; cf. Dan. 2.18, etc.) which was conveyed by God to Habakkuk, but whose meaning was concealed from him, would be given its 'interpretation' (Hebrew: *pesher*) by the Teacher of Righteousness who would show that the ancient prophecy was written with reference, not to the past, but to the people and the happenings of their own day. Dr F. F. Bruce has shown[1] that this same method of interpretation is in many respects similar to that adopted by the early Christians and that a number of passages in the New Testament can easily be translated into *pesher*-idiom in which the interpretation of

[1] *New Testament Studies*, vol. 2, no. 3, pp. 176ff, article on 'Qumran and Early Christianity'.

prophecy is given in terms of the writer's own day or in terms of the end of the age.[1]

Among the writings found at Qumran is one called 'The War of the Sons of Light against the Sons of Darkness' where plans are described for the execution of a Holy War which would usher in the time of the end. It seems certain that, at the time of the war with Rome (A.D. 66), in the spirit of this book, the Covenanters showed ready sympathy with the Zealots as a result of which their centre at Qumran was destroyed, as archaeological evidence indicates, in the year A.D. 68. And if, as seems likely, they are to be identified with a branch of the Essenes, this would explain the report of Josephus that at this time many of the Essenes were cruelly tortured.

The sects of Judaism differed from one another in many respects; but, Sadducees apart, they were bound together by one thing as by nothing else in their fight against the common foe; not devotion to party or even to fatherland, but to the sacred Torah and the holy Covenant of the Lord their God.

---

[1] He illustrates this by linking Hab. 1.5 with Acts 13.16ff as interpretation; Hab. 2.3f with Heb. 10.37f, Rom. 1.17 and Gal. 3.11; Amos 5. 25ff with Acts 7.42f; Ps. 95.10 with Heb. 3.9f.

3

The Sacred Writings

'OF making-many books there is no end; and much study is a weariness of the flesh' (Eccles. 12.12). These words no doubt have a timeless quality about them, but the writer probably had in mind books of Greek origin written at the beginning of the second century B.C. or a little later which reflected the prevailing Hellenistic culture of that time. These writings do not come within our immediate purview, but the quotation helps to remind us that within Palestine itself, from the first quarter of the second century B.C. right on into the first century A.D., there were also many Jewish writings, of diverse kinds, which had a lasting influence, if not on Judaism itself, then on Christianity, which claimed to be the 'new Israel' of God.

It has been the common practice to classify the literature of the Jews of this period as canonical, rabbinical, apocryphal and pseudepigraphal. But, as G. F. Moore has indicated,[1] such a classification was quite unknown to the Jews of that time and is indeed most misleading. A better classification, he suggests, would be that of canonical, 'normative' and 'extraneous' (or 'outside') books. By 'canonical' is meant that body of Holy Scripture acknowledged as authoritative; by 'normative' is meant the literature, or more correctly the oral tradition which ultimately found expression in literature, of rabbinical Judaism; and by 'extraneous' is meant those non-canonical

[1] *Op. cit.*, vol. 1, pp. 125ff.

writings to which the Rabbis gave the name 'the outside books'.

I. THE HOLY SCRIPTURES

A. *The Hebrew Canon*

According to Jewish usage the Hebrew Scriptures are divided into three groups known as *Torah* (Law), *Nebi'im* (Prophets—Former and Latter) and *Kethubim* (Hagiographa or Writings). These consist of twenty-four books which, by different division, appear in the Authorized Version as thirty-nine. Those books which were regarded as inspired and sacred and which carried 'canonical' authority were said by the Jews to 'make the hands unclean', a phrase whose origin is lost in obscurity but whose use 'was probably meant to prevent careless and irreverent handling of sacred books particularly by the priests'.[1] Not all the books of Holy Scripture were regarded as of equal authority, nor indeed were the three sections into which it was divided. They stood on three terraces, as it were, the highest place representing the Torah, the next the Prophets and the last the Writings.

From the time of Ezra onwards the Judaism which gradually developed attached the greatest possible importance to the revelation of the Torah given by God to Moses at Sinai and regarded the subsequent history as of far less importance; accordingly it was given a place apart as the supreme scriptural authority within the Jewish Church. It seems likely that by about 400-350 B.C. the Torah or Pentateuch, as we now have it, was completed; but it is more difficult to ascertain at what point it was regarded as having gained canonical authority. The kernel of the idea is perhaps to be found as far back as 621 B.C. when the reading of Josiah's Law Book (probably substantially our Deuteronomy) made such an impression on the people, and again in

[1] G. F. Moore, *ibid.*, vol. III, p. 66.

397 B.C. when Ezra's Law Book was read with similar effect. No doubt by about 350-300 B.C. the Pentateuch as a unit was revered by the people. But it was probably during the period 300-200 B.C., which as we have seen witnessed a gradual shifting of emphasis from the Temple to the Torah, that this body of Scripture came increasingly to have what we should call canonical authority. The Book of Tobit (c. 200 B.C.) shows great respect for the Torah, and Ben Sira (Ecclesiasticus) writing in 180 B.C. speaks of the Torah as the supreme gift of God and likens it to Wisdom (24.23), indicating that by this date at any rate it was regarded by Ben Sira as truly canonical. Thus, by about the year 200 B.C., or some time before, Torah religion was solidly based. In the light of this fact we can well understand the importance ascribed to the Temple Scrolls in the First Book of Maccabees where the implication is that the Torah must be defended even if the Temple be destroyed (cf. 1.56f; 2.26f, 48).

Further valuable information is given by Ben Sira concerning the formation of the second division of the Canon known as 'the Prophets'. In ch. 44ff, he gives a list of famous men mentioned in Scripture whose names are arranged in such a way and with such detail that we are led to the conclusion that the greater part of the Old Testament, as we now have it, was known to him at that time. He makes it clear that at least 'the Law' and 'the Prophets' were known to him and actually refers to 'the Twelve Prophets' as a definite collection. One factor which would facilitate the closing of this division of 'the Prophets' would be the belief then prevalent that from the time of Ezra onwards prophetic activity and prophetic inspiration had ceased (cf. I Macc. 4.46; 9.27; 14.41 and the Maccabean Ps. 74.9). By about 250-200 B.C., then, we may say that the division of 'the Prophets' was closed. This explains why such a book as Daniel is not to be found among 'the Prophets' but among 'the Writings', for Daniel was not written until about the year 165 B.C.

A clearly-defined landmark in tracing the idea of the Canon is given in the Prologue to Ben Sira which was composed by that writer's grandson about 132 B.C. He speaks there of the law, and the prophets, and the others who followed after them, and of 'the law itself, and the prophecies, and the rest of the books'. Such statements show that by this time other books were regarded as of special religious value and could be set in a class apart; they indicate that the three-fold division of Scripture was in existence but that the third section was still fluid and had not as yet acquired a distinctive name. This same conclusion is indicated by the evidence of Luke 24.44 which refers to what is written 'in the law of Moses, and the prophets, and the psalms', where again the last section is left undetermined. The author of II Esdras (c. A.D. 90) indicates that at that time there were probably twenty-four books standing in the Hebrew Scriptures (cf. 14.44ff) and this is also a justifiable inference from the evidence of the New Testament and of Josephus who, probably by a different grouping, gives the number as twenty-two. None of these sources, however, gives the technical name for the third section of Scripture. The first reference to the three sections together by their Hebrew names is by Rabbi Gamaliel, the same Gamaliel mentioned in Acts 5. We may draw the conclusion that by New Testament times at least the Canon of Scripture was virtually closed.

But for a long time to come controversy continued over a number of the books. In particular there had been dissension between the famous Schools of Hillel and Shammai over the position of the Song of Songs and Ecclesiastes.[1] A decision of the Council of Jamnia (c. A.D. 90) accepted the two books as canonical, thus supporting the School of Hillel. The Hebrew Scriptures

[1] These two books together with the book of Esther, are nowhere mentioned in the New Testament. For the influence of the apocryphal books on the New Testament and in the history of the Christian Church see pp. 88ff.

were then limited to twenty-four books (five in the Pentateuch, eight in the Prophets and eleven in the Writings) which correspond to the thirty-nine books of the Authorized Version. But division of opinion continued and the matter of the Canon was still a point of debate in the second and third centuries A.D. There was no definite time, then, when a deliberate collection was made of books called 'canonical'. Rather, by their contribution to the record of divine revelation and by their popularity and use in synagogue worship they gradually won for themselves an established position within the body of sacred Scripture.

B. *The Scriptures in the Dispersion*

We know that already, by about the year 250 B.C., the Pentateuch had been translated into Greek for the use of the Jews of the Dispersion, and the preface to the Greek version of Ben Sira indicates that by that date (132 B.C.) the Former and Latter Prophets had also been rendered into Greek. It is uncertain how many of 'the Writings' had been translated by, say, the beginning of the Christian Era or were regarded as canonical in Alexandria. No limit had as yet been placed on 'the rest of the books'.

The Greek Bible which emerged and which was ultimately to be taken over by the Christian Church was much less restricted than the Hebrew Scriptures and adopted a different ordering of the books. We know that the Christians regarded the so-called 'outside books' in rather a different light from the Jews in Palestine and continued to read them in Greek translation long

---

[1] Eusebius informs us (*Hist. Eccl.*, iv, 26) that Melito, Bishop of Sardis (d. A.D. 180), when asked what were the books in the Canon, confessed that he did not know but would make enquiries about the matter when he was in the east. This suggests that, at least in some parts of the Christian Church, there was still some doubt regarding the contents of the Canon. The books subsequently named by Melito were those of the Jewish Canon except the Book of Esther. He no doubt received his information from Christian Jews for whom Esther, with its stress on the nationalistic Feast of Purim, was of little significance.

after they had fallen out of favour in Palestine. Indeed they not only continued to copy them, but actually included certain of them in the Greek codices which contained their sacred Scriptures interspersed among 'the Writings' without, however, raising the issue whether they were to be regarded as canonical or not. Officially there could be only one Canon, viz. that of the Hebrew Scriptures, but in popular usage this strict interpretation would not always be followed, particularly as 'the Writings' themselves, as we have just seen, were as yet still in a fluid state. It is a fair assumption that, though they were regarded as sacred, they were not considered canonical in any true sense and were certainly on quite a different level of inspiration from either the Law or the Prophets. To refer to this larger body of Scripture as 'the Alexandrian Canon', as if it can be set over against the Palestinian Canon as something different, is really to beg the question. It is significant that Philo (died *c*. A.D. 50), a typical Alexandrian Jew, makes no mention of these non-canonical books, and by the time of Josephus the Greek Bible which he used consisted substantially of the books of the Hebrew Canon as we know it today.

2. THE ORAL TRADITION

During the inter-testamental period, as we have seen, the Torah became for the Jews the supreme religious authority and Judaism established itself as a religion of the Book. But as H. Wheeler Robinson reminds us, 'Every religion that builds on a book is compelled to devise means to reinterpret that book so as to adapt its original meaning to the changing needs of successive generations. Thus it came to pass that alongside of the written Torah there grew up a mass of interpretation, natural or artificial, which formed the unwritten Torah, "the tradition of the elders" (Mark 7.3).'[1]

[1] *A Companion to the Bible*, ed. by T. W. Manson, 1939, p. 313.

A. *Its origin and development*

The beginnings of this process of interpretation are to be found with the Sopherim who endeavoured to advance the aims of Ezra, the great 'founder of the Law'. Ezra is described as 'a ready scribe in the Torah of Moses' (Ezra 7.6) who had 'set his heart to interpret the Torah of the Lord and to do it' (Ezra 7.10). Not only did he 'read in the book, in the law of God, distinctly', he 'gave the sense and caused them to understand the reading' (Neh. 8.8). This is exactly what the Sopherim also sought to do. They set themselves the task not only of making the Torah the possession of the people, but of discovering and interpreting its meaning so that men could apply it to their daily lives. To them the Torah was much more than a survival from the glorious past with only an archaic value; it was a living oracle through which the word of God could come to generation after generation. Its word was not static but dynamic, capable of fresh interpretations for each succeeding age and capable of renewed application to every aspect of human life.

The method which they used in their teaching was of the nature of a running commentary on the words of Scripture. The particular custom or practice or precept which they sought to elucidate was brought into relation with a text or passage of Scripture which was then expounded and an interpretation given.[1] This method was known as the Midrash form (Hebrew *darash*, to interpret) and was a feature of the Sopherim's teaching.

In many places the teaching of the Torah, by precept and judgment, was perfectly clear both in its ethical and in its legal meanings; in such instances it was the duty of the Sopherim and their successors to impress this teaching on the minds of the

[1] One of the very rare surviving examples of this method is to be found in the Mishnah tractate *Sotah*, viii. 1, 2. Cf. Herbert Danby's translation of the Mishnah, 1933, pp. 301f, and R. Travers Herford, *op. cit.*, 1933, pp. 48f, where the passage is given in full.

people. In other places, however, the ruling of the Torah was not clear; then its meaning must be expounded and its truth applied. Sometimes, it is true, laws arising out of prevailing custom became established which could not find justification in the Torah, but authority would be given to them on the ground that they formed a 'fence round the Torah' (Pirke Aboth 1.1). This 'fence' consisted of cautionary rules, such as that forbidding not simply the use but even the handling of tools on the Sabbath day. Thus a man would be halted before he found himself within striking distance of a breach of the law of God. In such ways the Torah was made more and more the centre of the people's life.

This task, so well begun by the Sopherim, was continued and developed by teachers who later became the Rabbis and whose work did so much to fashion and determine the shape of Judaism in years to come. It is reported that the tradition of the Sopherim was passed on by Simon the Just to one Antigonus of Socho and that thereafter it was transmitted to a series of teachers whose names are given in pairs from Jose ben Joezer and Jose ben Johanan, who lived about 160 B.C., right down in line of succession to Hillel and Shammai in the time of Jesus (cf. Pirke Aboth 1.1-12). Like the Sopherim before them these teachers set themselves the task of interpreting the Torah to the people and of regulating their lives according to its guidance.

But during this period there took place a development, in connection with the status of extra-Scriptural laws, which was to have far-reaching effects. As we have seen, customs and traditions, chiefly of a religious nature, had arisen through the course of the years which had come to be accepted as authoritative within the practice of Judaism even although no justification for them could be found in the Torah. In due course the question came to be asked concerning the relation between the authority of this tradition and the authority of the written Torah. It was clear that there could not be two such independent authorities. And so there emerged the all-important belief that the Torah was more than simply the written word of Scripture, but included the tradition which had been handed down from generation to generation. The Torah of God was in two parts, written and oral, and each was of equal authority. Not only so; each was of equal antiquity, for Moses himself had received the Torah, written and oral, at Sinai whence it had been handed down through successive generations of faithful men (Pirke Aboth 1.1.). It was no doubt the formulation of this belief which led to the breach in the Sanhedrin in the time of John Hyrcanus (134-104 B.C.) and the appearance of the two parties of the Pharisees and Sadducees.[1] The Pharisees were staunch supporters of the authority of the oral tradition and were bitterly opposed by the Sadducees who, although they had their own ordinances relating to sacrificial matters and the like, regarded the written Torah as alone authoritative.

The dangers inherent in such a development as the unwritten Torah are obvious, especially when it became dissociated from the text of the written Torah and no longer needed to find its justification there. But it must be acknowledged that it rescued Judaism from that moribund state which must have been its fate had the nation followed the lead of the conservative Sadducees. By its means religion and life, work and worship, were integrated in a way impossible before, and God and his commandments were made real in the common life of the common people.

Its form and content

The rabbinical sources, in which the oral tradition has been Landed down but which remained oral throughout the inter-testamental period, divide themselves into two classes, the Midrash and the Mishnah.

The Sopherim and the teachers who succeeded them devoted

[1] See pp. 32 and 49f.

themselves, as we have seen,[1] to the exposition and application of the written Torah and, in the light of these studies, formed new regulations applicable to problems, ethical and legal, which would arise as life became more and more complex. This process was called *darash* (or 'interpretation'), and Midrash (or 'Exegesis') is the process of seeking out, of enquiring into, the written text to discover its implications.

This *Midrash* was divided into two sections. First, there was the Halakah (Hebrew *halak*, to walk) which consisted of regulations concerning matters of civil and religious law. It showed the way a man should *walk* by making clear how he could obey the Law in every detail. It was an exegesis of biblical laws out of which could be formed authoritative regulations for the life of the people. It is this Halakah which forms the oral tradition or unwritten Torah of Judaism.

Secondly, there was the Haggadah (Hebrew root *nagad*, to tell) or 'recounting'. This is that part of rabbinical literature which is not Halakah, i.e. anything which is not a point of law. It is a development, as it were, of the biblical stories rather than the biblical law. It contains a great deal of legend and odds and ends of Israelite folk-lore. But beside this there is a considerable amount of ethical and religious material. It refers often to the discourses of preachers in the Synagogues and teachers in the Schools and often mentions them by name. This haggadic material was very highly valued, but it did not have the authority in Judaism held by the halakic Midrash.

The Midrash was the concern of the Rabbis before the destruction of the second Temple, and after that date it became their main preoccupation. The function, presentation and amplification of the oral tradition were the main features of their studies. Their task then, as always, was to study the written Torah with its oral tradition and to transmit it to others. This process of study, the

[1] On pp. 64f.

repetition of the written Torah with its oral tradition, was called *shanah* or 'repetition', and the sum of the repetition was known as *Mishnah*.[1]

This word *Mishnah* is the name given to the second rabbinical source. It has been described as 'a systematic (topical) classification of the discussions and decisions of Rabbis during the previous centuries as to the right interpretation and expansion of the Torah'.[2] It is a code of law consisting of Halakah, with occasional haggadic elements, whose formation and codification came about in this way. After the fall of the Temple in A.D. 70, instead of elaborating a verse of Scripture at a time, the Rabbis began to arrange the *halakot* (plural of *halakah*), or individual religious laws of a practical kind, in a special order according to subject and not according to the biblical text. A lead in this matter was given by Johanan ben Zakkai and his disciples at Jamnia. At the beginning of the second century Rabbi Akiba (d. A.D. 135) ordered the *halakot* into a more elaborate form, though still orally. His pupil, Rabbi Meir (after A.D. 135) elaborated it again and cleared up dubious points. Then Rabbi Judah (the Patriarch), who died just after A.D. 200, made a final recension of the Mishnah, though we do not know if he actually wrote it down. Alterations were made after his day, but in the main it is the result of his work. In its written form it is divided into six orders according to subject-matter, each order containing a number of tractates (63 in all) and can be dated about A.D. 200-230. After the Bible, the Mishnah is the ground-work of Jewish literature to our own day and is the foundation of the Talmud.[3] With the writing of

[1] In Aramaic *shanah* becomes *t*e*na'*. The Rabbis of the first two centuries A.D. who were engaged in this repetition of the Mishnah were known, and are still known, as *Tanna'im*.

[2] H. Wheeler Robinson, *op. cit.*, pp. 313f.

[3] The Talmud (lit. 'learning') is a compilation consisting of the Mishnah, or accepted body of traditional law, together with the subsequent discussions or traditions (the *Gemara*, lit. 'completion') concerning it which arose in the Jewish 'schools'. There are two Talmuds, the

the Mishnah the Jews were established as 'the people of the Book'.

3. THE 'OUTSIDE BOOKS'

A. *The non-canonical literature*

Mention has already been made of the fact that during the inter-testamental period there grew up, chiefly in Palestine, but also in the Dispersion, a fairly extensive Jewish literature which is of significance not only for Judaism but even more for Christianity.[1] On the one hand it gives interesting insights into the history of the Jews and the religion of Judaism outside the rabbinical Schools, and on the other hand it casts light upon the origins of the Christian faith. It is difficult to say how widespread these books were, but it would appear that their number was quite considerable.

The name given to them in rabbinical literature is *hisonim* meaning 'external' or 'outside' and signifies those books which lie outside the Canon of accepted Scripture. A clue to their identity is given in the Tosefta tractate, *Yadaim* ii. 13, which reads, 'The books [*sic*] of Ben Sira and all books which were written from then onwards do not defile the hands', i.e. are not canonical. The literature here referred to is presumably that whole group to which Ben Sira itself belongs, viz. the apocryphal and cognate literature (including many writings of an apocalyptic kind). In the Mishnah tractate, *Sanhedrin* x. 1, it is reported by the influential Rabbi Akiba (*c*. A.D. 132) that among those who have 'no share in the world to come' is 'he that reads the outside books'. On the surface this might be taken to mean that the reading of all such non-canonical books was forbidden, but in fact the reference

Palestinian and the Babylonian. In common usage reference is usually to the Babylonian Talmud which is fuller than the Palestinian. It acquired substantially its present shape about A.D. 500.

[1] See p. 16.

is presumably to the public *recitation* of them both in the liturgy of worship and in the discipline of study.

On what grounds was this literature considered non-canonical? W. D. Davies has suggested[1] four criteria determining the acceptance or rejection of any book:

i. The view that prophecy had ceased from Israel after Daniel in the Persian period, and that, therefore, all books written after that time could not be considered.

ii. The congruity of the contents of any book with the Torah (cf. discussions on the canonicity of Ezekiel).

iii. A certain self-consistency within the books concerned.

iv. The originally Hebrew character of any book.

These factors explain the inclusion of Daniel in the Canon and the exclusion of such books as Ecclesiasticus (or Ben Sira), Judith, Psalms of Solomon and I and II Maccabees. They explain also the exclusion of the Jewish apocalyptic writings which for some time had a measure of popularity among the Jews of Palestine. But there were probably additional reasons why the apocalyptic writings in particular were not accepted within the Canon of Scripture. One was the antipathy of the Rabbis who remembered the part played by such books in fanning the flames of revolt which led to the fall of Jerusalem in A.D. 70. That catastrophe and the subsequent reorganization of Judaism would lead to a concentration upon the Torah and its accompanying oral tradition. Coupled with this was the use which the Christians were beginning to make of this type of literature. They found the teaching of these books, particularly with respect to the Messiah, most suitable for their own ends; Christian interpolations began to be made in Jewish apocalyptic works and independent Christian apocalyptic writings appeared. All these

[1] *Expository Times*, vol. LIX, no. 9, June 1948.

factors together militated against the study and continued publication of such books on the part of the Jews. Among the last of the 'outside books' of an apocalyptic character to be written were II Esdras (i.e. 4 Ezra) 3-14 and the Apocalypse of Baruch about the year A.D. 90.

The majority of these books were written either in Hebrew (the language of the learned of that day) or in Aramaic (the vernacular and the language of Jewish literature generally), but, with the exception of Ecclesiasticus (or Ben Sira), they have survived only in translations, first into Greek and then into other languages. Some scholars, like C. C. Torrey, have argued that after A.D. 70 the decision was taken 'to destroy, systematically and thoroughly, the Semitic originals of all the extra-canonical literature. . . . The popular literature, which had had such a flourishing existence, was now discontinued as far as Palestinian Jewry was concerned.'[1] It is very doubtful, however, whether the evidence can lend itself to such an unqualified statement, for the divorce between Pharisaism and the ideas enshrined in apocalyptic was not anything like as complete as such an assertion would have us believe. But the antipathy towards apocalyptic of at least many of the Rabbis cannot be denied and, under their influence, these 'outside books' fell out of favour in Palestine.

Prior to this, however, they had been translated into Greek by the Jews of the Dispersion and had become very popular among the people there. Indeed, when they arrived in Alexandria they really came into their own and received a much wider circulation than they had ever had in Palestine. When, in course of time, the Jews of the Dispersion came to relinquish their hold on these writings they had already become the possession of the Christian Church through its adoption of the Septuagint with which certain of the 'outside books' had become incorporated. And so although in the first instance they were preserved by

[1] *The Apocryphal Literature*, 1945, p. 15.

Greek-speaking Jews in Egypt, it was the Christian Church which was ultimately responsible for their survival.

It is not surprising that the 'outside books', and in particular the apocalyptic writings among them, were from the beginning popular with the early Christians who had themselves been brought up in the Jewish faith; their relevance for the teaching of the Church concerning the imminent return of Christ was obvious. As more and more Gentiles flocked into the Church and as Aramaic gave way to Greek as the language of the Christian community their use would become even more widespread. With the exception of the canonical book of Daniel the tradition of apocalyptic is Christian and not Jewish. The numerous versions of II (4) Esdras indicates what a deep and widespread influence this body of teaching continued to have on the thinking of Christian people. Within Judaism the apocalyptic tradition, which had deeply influenced at least a section of the people from the time of Antiochus IV onwards in every recurring crisis, in due course ceased to exist.

B. *The milieu of apocalyptic*

It has been suggested above that the division between apocalyptic and orthodox Pharisaic Judaism was not as complete as some scholars have made it out to be. The differences between them cannot, of course, be denied; but the fact is that apocalyptic shared certain fundamental beliefs with rabbinical Judaism which gave them definite points of contact. For one thing they both adopted the same attitude towards the written Torah which each reverenced as the revelation of God. The centrality of the Torah in the thought of the apocalyptists can be illustrated from book after book, from Jubilees and the Testaments of the XII Patriarchs in the second century B.C. right up to 2 Baruch and II Esdras in the first century A.D. It is true that the form of apocalyptic differs considerably from the Halakah form of rabbinical literature,[1] but the evidence of such a book as Jubilees amply illustrates that this difference was by no means absolute in every case. The author of Jubilees is certainly familiar with the rabbinical method and produces evidence of *halakot* earlier even than those in the rabbinical sources themselves. Again, the apocalyptic element in these writings is frequently accompanied by a deep ethical concern which in many respects is the key to the understanding and appreciation of rabbinical Judaism. Then there is the eschatological outlook of these two groups of writings which, though dissimilar in many respects, reveals no small measure of agreement. This is most clearly seen in certain rabbinical expectations such as the resurrection of the body and the advent of the Messiah. A case in point is that of Rabbi Akiba who, as we have seen, at the beginning of the second century, elaborated and gave order to the *halakot*; it was this same man who eagerly awaited the coming of the Messiah and gave his whole-hearted support to the claims of Bar Kochba in his revolt in A.D. 132-135.

But this type of literature would perhaps appeal much more to the Zealots and those who shared their religious and political point of view. They would find a great deal here which would meet with their enthusiastic approval and would fire that nationalistic zeal by which they sought to bring to its fulfilment, if need be by the power of the sword, the revealed will of God. Our knowledge of the Essenes is limited and what we do know of them indicates that their beliefs would not always tally with those expressed in the apocalyptic writings. But the term may well designate a number of different groups whose beliefs and practices might well correspond more accurately to those of the apocalyptic literature. If the argument can be substantiated that the Covenanters of Qumran were in fact a branch of the Essenes, then the argument for the possible Essene influence on this type of

[1] See p. 67.

literature can perhaps be given greater credence than before, for the messianic and apocalyptic thought of the Dead Sea Scrolls has much in common with the apocalyptic writings in the 'outside books'.

In conclusion, the existence of this non-canonical literature, apocalyptic and otherwise, substantiates the point made earlier that during the inter-testamental period Judaism was a complex system containing within itself many sects, parties and types, for the literature itself discloses many different outlooks, interests and beliefs which cannot always be identified with any one of the recognized parties within Judaism. As R. Travers Herford says, 'The existence of writers such as those of the Apocryphal books points rather to complexity than simplicity in the literary activities of the time. Also, that the presence of many elements in the contemporary Judaism by no means implies that there was close interaction and mutual influence between them.'[1] To a closer examination of this 'apocryphal' literature we now turn.

[1] *Op. cit.*, p. 197.

4

The Apocryphal Literature

IN common parlance the word 'apocryphal' often carries with it the sense of 'false' or 'spurious', but in its origin and in its ecclesiastical usage the meaning is altogether different. There it carries the same meaning as the Hebrew expression 'outside books' and refers to those books which lie outside the Canon of Scripture. Etymologically the word 'apocrypha' (plural of Greek *apocryphon*) designates things withdrawn from the eyes, hidden or secret. It has been suggested[1] that the reason why the 'outside books' came to be called 'hidden (books)' is to be found in certain references in II Esdras. There Ezra is bidden to re-write all the sacred books of Israel which had been destroyed. Twenty-four of these (the canonical books) he had to publish, and seventy (the 'outside books') he had to *hide* (cf. 14.6, 45ff). These 'hidden' or 'apocryphal' books, whilst lying outside the Canon, were nevertheless of great value within the Jewish tradition represented by this writer.

In more modern usage, however, the word has a much more restricted reference. Among Protestants it is generally used to describe those books which are to be found in the Christian Greek and Latin Bibles (i.e. the Septuagint and the Vulgate), but which are not found in the Hebrew Bible; here the word 'pseudepigrapha' is frequently used to refer to the rest of the 'outside books', of indeterminate number, which lie outside the canonical

[1] Cf. C. C. Torrey, *op. cit.*, pp. 8f.

Scriptures and the 'Apocrypha' and which, for some considerable time, were widely read in the oriental and other branches of the early Christian Church. In Roman Catholic usage the word 'deuterocanonical' is given to those books described by Protestants as 'apocryphal', and the word 'apocryphal' is given to those known as 'pseudepigraphal'. Where, for the sake of convenience, a distinction must be made, the Protestant usage will here be adopted.

I. THE BOOKS COMMONLY CALLED 'THE APOCRYPHA'

A. *Their identity*

The books of the Old Testament Apocrypha are best known to the modern reader as they appear in the Authorized Version, where they are gathered together to form a block of literature between the Old and New Testaments. They are twelve in number of which one (II Esdras) is not found in the Greek Septuagint but appears in the Vulgate.

  i. I Esdras.
 ii. II Esdras.
iii. Tobit.
 iv. Judith.
  v. The Rest of the chapters of the Book of Esther.
 vi. The Wisdom of Solomon.
vii. The Wisdom of Jesus the son of Sirach,[1] or Ecclesiasticus.
viii. Baruch (with the Epistle of Jeremy as chapter 6).[2]
 ix. The Additions to Daniel:

   (*a*) The Song of the Three Holy Children
   (*b*) The History of Susanna
   (*c*) Bel and the Dragon.

[1] This is the form the name takes in Greek. The Hebrew form 'Ben Sira' (son of Sira) is used throughout this book.
[2] The RSV Apocrypha separates the Epistle of Jeremy from Baruch. In some Greek codices they are separated by another book.

x. The Prayer of Manasses.
xi. I Maccabees.
xii. II Maccabees.

With the exception of I Esdras (before 200 B.C.) and II Esdras (*c.* A.D. 90) these books were composed during the last two centuries B.C., for the most part in Palestine. Only two of the authors are known to us by name, Jesus (Hebrew, Joshua; Aramaic, Jeshua) the son of Sirach[1] (Ecclus. 50.27) and Jason of Cyrene whose five books are summarized in II Maccabees 3-15 (II Macc. 2.23).

Although all of them became popular in the Greek language, only a very small number were originally written in that tongue. These are II Maccabees 2.19-15.39, the Wisdom of Solomon and the decrees of Ahasuerus in Esther 13.1-7 and 16.1-24. All the rest were composed either in Hebrew (Baruch, Ben Sira, I Maccabees, Judith, the Prayer of Manasses and probably the Song of the Three Holy Children) or in the popular Aramaic (II Macc. 1.1-2.18, the Story of the Three Youths in I Esdras 3.1-4.63, Tobit, the Rest of Esther 10.4-13; 11.2-12.6; 13.8-18; 14.1-19; 15.1-16, the History of Susanna, Bel and the Dragon, the Epistle of Jeremy, II Esdras).

NOTE ON THE BOOKS OF ESDRAS

The titles and order of these books differ in the various versions:

The English Versions (since the Geneva Bible, 1560)	*The Vulgate*	*The Septuagint*
Ezra	First Esdras	Esdras B, chs. 1-10
Nehemiah	Second Esdras	Esdras B, chs. 11-23
I Esdras	Third Esdras	Esdras A
II Esdras	Fourth Esdras	[not in Greek]

[1] See p. 76, n.1.

B. *Their contents and literary genre*

The literature represented in 'the Apocrypha' is of a varied character ranging from history to poetry, from fiction to philosophy, from legend to lectures on the good life. Some of it was written to edify, some to reprove, and some perhaps simply to entertain. Whatever its purpose it is worth reading for its own sake.

History is well represented by I Maccabees which, written on the pattern of the canonical Books of Kings, gives a trustworthy account of the Jews in Palestine from the years before the Maccabean Revolt until the death of Simon (175-134 B.C.). The book breathes an indomitable faith in the purpose of God for the community of Israel and sees in the House of the Maccabees his instrument of salvation. II Maccabees, which covers a shorter period (176-161 B.C.), is quite independent of I Maccabees and is less trustworthy, having a goodly proportion of legend mingled with history. It was written in Greek in Alexandria about 50 B.C. and shows a zeal for the Temple and for the strict observance of the Law of Moses (cf. the moving stories of the martyrdom of Eleazar in 6.18-31 and the Seven Brothers in 7.1-42).

Legend is illustrated by II Macc. 1.1-2.18 which purports to be the contents of two letters sent in 124 B.C. and 143 B.C. from Jews in Palestine to Jews in Egypt. The second of these tells how Jeremiah commanded the priests, when they were about to be led into captivity, to hide the sacred altar fire in the hollow of a well; in the time of Nehemiah search was made for it and in its stead a black liquid was found which ignited with the heat of the sun and consumed the sacrifice. This liquid the people called 'naphtha'. The same letter tells how Jeremiah gave the exiles the law and urged them to keep it, and how he hid the tabernacle, the ark and the altar of incense in a cave in Mount Nebo.

Fiction is well represented in this literature and contains some stories of Gentile origin. Only one of these books (Judith) was written in Hebrew; the rest were in the vernacular Aramaic. The Book of Judith (meaning 'Jewess') is a thrilling story in the style of the Song of Deborah (Judges 5) of how one Judith delivered her people from the hands of Holofernes, who, falling prey to wine and women, quite literally lost his head to a charming widow!

The Story of the Three Youths (probably of Persian origin) in I Esdras 3.1-5.3 is one of the finest tales in this literature from the point of view of style and literary eloquence. It tells of three young guardsmen in the service of Darius, King of Persia, who challenged one another to a competition. They had to write down what, in their opinion, was the strongest thing in the world and had to argue their case before the king. The first wrote, 'Wine is the strongest'; the second, 'The King is the strongest'; and the third, 'Women are strongest, but above all things truth beareth away the victory.' The survival of the work we call I Esdras was largely due to the popularity which this story had among the Christians who inherited it from the Jews.

The Book of Tobit must have ranked high among the 'best-sellers' of the day. It is a first-rate 'short story' with a fine plot well executed. It was written about 200 B.C. probably by an Egyptian or a Babylonian Jew and is influenced by certain Gentile writings, although its entire moral and spiritual outlook is shaped by the Old Testament Scriptures. The story tells of a Jew named Tobit in Nineveh, who sent his son Tobias on an errand to Media accompanied by Azarias (the angel Raphael in disguise). There they met and helped one Sara whose seven husbands had been slain by the demon Asmodeus, each on his wedding night. Tobias and Sara are married and live happily ever after!

The History of Susanna and the Stories of Bel and the Dragon are in the true 'detective story' tradition. Susanna, the beautiful wife of a Babylonian Jew, resisted the advances of two elderly judges whose intentions were none too honourable, whereupon they threatened to 'frame' her by alleging 'an affair' with a young man. She was condemned to death. But Daniel demanded a new trial in which the two judges were shown to give contradictory evidence. Susanna was acquitted and the judges put to death.

The Story of Bel is a polemic against heathen gods and against idolatry generally. Daniel, we are told, refused to worship Bel and maintained that the loads of food and drink which the priests provided for the god each day were not eaten by him. Cyrus bade his priests prove their case. Confidently they set the food and drink in order and sealed the doors, for they had a secret entrance underneath the table! But Daniel 'went one better' and secretly scattered ashes on the temple floor before the doors were shut. In the morning the food and drink were gone and the priests were jubilant. But the footprints of men, women and children on the ashes gave the game away! The priests and their families were slain and the idol and its temple destroyed.

Psalms and Hymns, several of which are scattered throughout these books, are illustrated in the Song of the Three Holy Children which consists of two poems separated by a short prose section. The first poem gives the prayer of Azarias, who, together with his two companions, praised God in the midst of the fiery furnace; the second is a song of praise from the lips of the 'three children' to the God who had delivered them from death.

Wisdom literature is represented by two very important books, the Wisdom of Solomon and the Wisdom of Ben Sira. The Wisdom of Solomon, written in epigrammatic style, was composed by an Alexandrian Jew (or Jews) perhaps in the early part of the first century B.C. and is quite unique among the apocryphal writings in the way in which it combines Jewish religion with Greek philosophy.[1] It is impossible to summarize its contents in brief, but these indicate two objectives—first to win back apostate

---

[1] See pp. 17, 23f.

Jews and to establish pious Jews in their faith, and secondly to demonstrate to the heathen in a language and thought they could understand the truth of Judaism and the folly of paganism. The writer exhorts his readers to seek after righteousness, for thus is wisdom found.

The Wisdom of Ben Sira is perhaps the most important book in 'the Apocrypha' for the light it sheds on the religion and life of the Jews in Palestine around the year 180 B.C. when it was composed. It is a digest of lectures the author gave in his School at Jerusalem in which he sought to impart to his pupils the wisdom of the ancients, that they might live 'according to the Law'. Again, it is impossible here to summarize in brief the topics with which he deals. They are taken from the synagogue, the home, the school and the work-a-day world. His advice ranges from points of etiquette to the life of communion with God ordained in his holy Law—behaviour at table, bringing up children, self-control, helping the poor, greed, the worship of mammon, true piety and much more besides. All this advice he sums up in the word 'wisdom' which is God's guide for the whole of life.

Apocalyptic is represented here by II Esdras 3-13, to which chapter 14 has been added by another hand. The book is an account of six visions given by God to 'Ezra'. These have been described as 'an apocalyptic drama in two acts: the "tying of the knot", in the present age (visions 1-3); and the "denouement" in the world to come (visions 4-6)'.[1] It was written probably about the year A.D. 90 and reflects the disillusionment which followed the destruction of Jerusalem twenty years before. Men's only hope was in the new age which would yet be born. A fuller treatment of the significance of this book will be reserved for a later point when the apocalyptic literature as a whole will be considered.[2]

---

[1] R. H. Pfeiffer in *The Interpreter's Bible*, vol. I, 1952, p. 399.
[2] See ch 5.

c. *Their historical and religious value*

Reference has already been made to the value of I Maccabees as an indispensable source for the history of the second century B.C. and consequently for the religious beliefs and practices of the period with which it deals. But many of the other books besides have an important contribution to make in this same connection and together give an invaluable picture of Jewish life and religion in the years preceding the birth of Christianity.

Respect for *the Temple* in Jerusalem is shown not only in the historical narratives (e.g. I Macc. 7.37), but elsewhere as in the Book of Tobit it is held in high esteem and approval is given to pilgrimages to Jerusalem and payment of tithes in the Temple there (1.4-8; 5.13). In Ben Sira, too, the Temple rites (cf. 35.4ff) and the Aaronic priesthood (45.6ff) are honoured and in particular the High Priest Simeon is extolled (50.1ff).

Complementary to the Temple was the sacred *Torah*, whose place and prestige were to become greater as the years passed by. Tobit, for example, lays stress on obedience to the Law of Moses, whilst in Ben Sira, as we have seen, the Torah is described as the very epitome of Wisdom itself (24.23). Already the foundation was being laid for the time when the Jews would be willing to die in defence of the blessed Torah (cf. I Macc. 2.27).

Throughout these writings stress is laid on the importance of *legalistic requirements*. Tobit, for example, refers to purification after contact with a corpse, washing before meals, observing the feasts, rendering the priestly dues and supporting orphans, widows and proselytes. In particular almsgiving is regarded as a sacred duty to be practised by rich and poor alike. Ample evidence is given in I Maccabees of the great importance of the rite of circumcision (cf. 1.15, 48; 2.46) and the observance of the Sabbath (2.34, 41). Another observance almost equally important is that of laws relating to food. Tobit tells us that when he was carried away captive to Nineveh he refused to eat 'the bread of the Gentiles' (1.10-11). Judith, too, refused to take the food and the wine which Holofernes offered her (12.2). Indeed, the success of her plan to deliver the nation, it would seem, depended upon her fulfilling the law even to the smallest detail of dietary observance (8.4-6; 12.1-9; cf. also II Macc. 6.18-7.1). The religious outlook of the Jews is summed up in these words of Baruch, 'This is the book of the commandments of God, and the law that endureth for ever. All they that hold it fast are destined for life, but such as leave it shall die' (Baruch 4.1).

But legalism was not the only thing which Torah religion fostered. It encouraged in many *a deep personal piety* which found expression in *good works* and in service to others. All through the Book of Tobit, for example, there is a sense of reverence and respect shown to parents which indicates a true spirit of piety prevailing in many Jewish family circles at that time; in particular the prayers of Tobit and of Sara for deliverance from their troubles are no doubt typical of many prayers of their day. Ben Sira, too, breathes the spirit of prayer in several passages which closely resemble the Psalms in their devotional atmosphere (cf. 2.1-18; 17.24-18.14; 22.27-23.6). His religious outlook is well summed up in these words:

> 'Riches and strength will lift up the heart;
> And the fear of the Lord is above both:
> There is nothing wanting in the fear of the Lord,
> And there is no need to seek help therein' (40.26).

He who observes the Law does as much in God's eyes as if he offered many sacrifices:

> 'He that keepeth the law multiplieth offerings;
> He that taketh heed to the commandments sacrificeth a peace offering.
> He that requiteth a good turn offereth fine flour;

And he that giveth alms sacrificeth a thank-offering' (35.1-2).

The multiplying of offerings is not enough:

'The Most High hath no pleasure in the offerings of the ungodly;
Neither is he pacified for sins by the multitude of sacrifices'
(34.19).

This whole passage, indeed, breathes the spirit of Amos, requiring mercy for the poor and justice for the oppressed (cf. 4.1-6; 34.18-26).

During this whole period a great development took place in the Jewish conception of *the last things* and this too is illustrated in these writings. In Baruch, for example, the promise is given to the Jewish people that they will see their triumph over their enemies and God will restore them to their own land (2.30-35, etc.). Tobit declares that the time will come when Jerusalem will be rebuilt and the Temple will be restored to its former glory and even beyond; the tribes will assemble once again in Jerusalem and the heathen will worship the Lord as their God (13.1ff; 14.4-7). In both these books reference is made to the eschatology of the nation, but none to the eschatology of the individual. It is to the apocalyptists, represented in 'the Apocrypha' by II Esdras 3-13, that we owe a synthesis of these two eschatologies through their belief in a doctrine of resurrection from the dead. Under their influence the writer of II Maccabees, for example, expresses his belief in the resurrection of the just who will be raised from the dead to inherit eternal life (7.9, 11, 14, 23, 29, 36; 12.43-45). In this he differs from another Alexandrian book, the Wisdom of Solomon, which, under the influence of Greek thought, teaches the immortality of the soul (2.23; 3.4; 5.15; 6.18; 8.17; 15.3). This teaching of Wisdom, together with its belief in the pre-existence of the soul (8.19-20) which becomes imprisoned in the 'corruptible body' (9.15), is foreign not only to Hebrew thought but also to

Jewish apocalyptic expectations.[1] The apocalyptists stood in the line of Hebrew tradition and, through their spiritual insights, prepared the way for Christianity, not only in its doctrine of the resurrection, but in its belief in the Kingdom of God and of the Messiah who would one day come to reign.

2. THE OTHER 'APOCRYPHAL' BOOKS (OR THE PSEUDEPIGRAPHA)

A. *Their identity*

There is no agreed list of those other apocryphal books which lie outside 'the Apocrypha' and to which the name 'pseudepigrapha' is sometimes given. They represent several types of literature, but undoubtedly the most common and the most important is that of apocalyptic. Some of them are apocalypses, properly so called, whilst others, though not predominantly apocalyptic, have quite considerable apocalyptic elements in them. Indeed there are few, if any, which do not come into this category. An account of their method and their teaching will be given later. Here we note a list of such books generally accepted as belonging to this classification together with their approximate dates of composition.

With a Palestinian origin:

    i. I Enoch 6-36, 37-71, 83-90, 91-104 (*c*. 164 B.C.).
    ii. The Book of Jubilees (*c*. 150 B.C.).
    iii. The Testaments of the Twelve Patriarchs (140-110 B.C.).
    iv. The Psalms of Solomon (*c*. 50 B.C.).
    v. The Testament of Job (first century B.C.).
    vi. The Assumption of Moses (A.D. 7-28).
    vii. The Lives of the Prophets (first century A.D.).
    viii. The Martyrdom of Isaiah (A.D. 1-50).

[1] See pp. 24f.

   ix. The Testament of Abraham (A.D. 1-50).
    x. The Apocalypse of Abraham 9-32 (A.D. 70-100).
   xi. II Baruch or the Apocalypse of Baruch (A.D. 50-100).
  xii. The Life of Adam and Eve or the Apocalypse of Moses
      (A.D. 80-100).

With a Hellenistic origin:

 xiii. The Sibylline Oracles: Book III (150-120 B.C.).
                       Book IV (*c.* A.D. 80).
                       Book V (before A.D. 130).
  xiv. III Maccabees (near end of first century B.C.).
   xv. IV Maccabees (near end of first century B.C. or beginning
      of first century A.D.).
  xvi. II Enoch or the Book of the Secrets of Enoch (A.D. 1-50).
 xvii. III Baruch (A.D. 100-175).

B. *In the Qumran Community*

This number of books has been considerably augmented by the discoveries at Qumran near the shores of the Dead Sea. Among the thousands of fragments found there are many of an apocryphal, and in particular an apocalyptic, character; some are written in Hebrew and others in Aramaic and others, it is reported, in a secret writing. It would appear that these writings were very popular among the members of the Qumran community and it may be that some of them were actually written there.

Many fragments of apocalyptic writings related to the Book of Enoch have come to light, written in Hebrew and Aramaic. One of these has much in common with I Enoch 94-103, with its account of admonitions to the righteous and woes to the sinners, and refers on several occasions to the 'future secret'[1] by whose means the mysteries of this present age will at last be revealed. This is a fairly common idea in apocalyptic as, for example, in

---

[1] See pp. 56, 95ff, 105.

II Esdras. Another set of fragments contain an account of the birth of Noah, known previously only in I Enoch 106. It is possible that these are part of a long-lost writing, the so-called 'Book of Noah', recognized by many to be one of the sources of the Book of Enoch.[1] Yet another collection of fragments, written in Aramaic, have been found which describe a vision of the New Jerusalem and show a particular interest in the Temple and its cult.[2] The indication is that this writing must have been very popular among the Covenanters because the fragments represent a number of copies and were discovered in several of the Qumran caves. Fragments have also been found of the Book of Jubilees, an Aramaic Testament of Levi (believed to be a source of the Testaments of the Twelve Patriarchs) and a Hebrew Testament of Naphtali.

Writings of a haggadic[3] character have also come to light among the Qumran scrolls. Parts of a work similar to the Book of Jubilees, for example, have been found which may be a source of that book or a later recension of it, or perhaps they may represent an independent writing, for it seems to advocate a calendar differing in some ways from that of Jubilees itself. Of considerable interest are forty-nine fragments of a Hebrew writing which seems to follow the Book of Deuteronomy in somewhat the same way as Jubilees does the Book of Genesis. Because of this it is generally known as 'The Little Deuteronomy' or 'The Words of Moses'. It is just possible that we have here an apocryphal history of the patriarchs or even a hitherto unknown document, 'The Wars of the Patriarchs', which is one of the sources of Jubilees (cf. 34.1-9) and the Testaments of the Twelve Patriarchs (cf. Testament of Judah 3-7).

[1] Cf. I Enoch 6-11; 54.7-55.2; 60; 65.1-69.25; 106-107. Portions of this 'Noachic literature' may also have been preserved in Jubilees 7.20-39; 10.1-15.
[2] The editors have given it the title 'The Description of the New Jerusalem'.
[3] See p. 67.

Of interest also is an Aramaic paraphrase of Genesis 5-15 which adorns the biblical narrative with haggadic comments on the text and has much in common with our apocalyptic literature.[1] Fragments of other haggadic narrative books have also much in common with writings ascribed to Jeremiah and Baruch, but which cannot be identified with any writings already known to us. Of particular interest is a pseudo-historical writing set in the Persian period, which recalls the books of Esther and Daniel.

3. THE APOCRYPHAL BOOKS IN CHRISTIANITY

A. *In the New Testament*

It is fairly obvious from a reading of the New Testament that its writers and its readers in the earliest days were familiar with at least some of the apocryphal books, not only those which they inherited from the Jews in the Septuagint, but also with the wider range of writings. The clearest reference is to be found in Jude, verses 14-16, where a quotation, no doubt from memory, is given from Enoch 1.9 recounting a prophecy of 'that Enoch in the seventh generation from Adam'. Apart from this more or less direct quotation there are many allusions made to the apocryphal literature. The words, 'Women received their dead by a resurrection: and others were tortured, not accepting their deliverance', recorded in Heb. 11.35, remind us of the martyrdom of Eleazar and the Seven Brothers in II Maccabees 6 and 7, and 'they were sawn asunder' in Heb. 11.37 is no doubt an allusion to the Martyrdom of Isaiah, whilst the phrases 'the effulgence of his glory' and 'the very image of his substance' in Heb. 1.3 remind us forcibly of the Book of Wisdom 7.26. Echoes of the Book of Wisdom are probably to be heard also in the words of the chief priest concerning the dying Jesus in Matt. 27.43, 'Let him deliver him now,

[1] This writing was at first thought to be a copy of the Book of Lamech to which reference is made in a few ancient lists.

if he desireth him: for he said, I am the Son of God' (cf. Wisd. 2.18); so also in Paul's letters such as Rom. 1.20-32 (Wisd. 14. 22-31), Rom. 9.21 (Wisd. 15.7), II Cor. 5.4 (Wisd. 9.15) and Eph. 6.13-17 (Wisd. 5.18-20). Again, certain sentiments and phrases familiar to the Christian reader in the Gospels have their near-parallels in the Testaments of the Twelve Patriarchs, expressions like forgiving one's neighbour (Matt. 18.21, cf. Test. of Gad 6.3, 7), loving with the whole heart (Matt. 22.37-39, cf. Test. of Dan 5.3), and returning good for evil (Luke 6.27f, cf. Test. of Joseph 8.2). These show how close the contents of Jesus' moral teaching were at times to the moral ideals of Judaism.

The dispute between Michael and the devil for the body of Moses in Jude 9 derives from the Assumption of Moses, and the doctrine of the 'imprisoned spirits' in I Peter 3.19 is drawn from Enoch 14-15. The Epistle of James has much in common with the apocryphal books; the writer was no doubt familiar with Ben Sira whose store of thought and experience he shared (cf., for example, James 1.19 and Ben Sira 5.11). References are made in the New Testament to unknown writings (cf. I Cor. 2.9; Eph. 5.14; I Tim. 3.16) and quotations are given from unknown sources (Matt. 23.34, 35; cf. Luke 11.49-51), whilst in one place (II Tim. 3.8) allusion is made to Jannes and Jambres whose names were taken for the title of an apocryphal book known to us from later writings.

No doubt the early Christians found these books religiously edifying, not only in their private devotions, but also in their training of catechumens. The question of canonicity would not enter at this point at all. That problem was yet to be raised and settled by the growing Church.

B. *In the history of the Church*

Among the early Church Fathers the books of 'the Apocrypha' were generally regarded as part of sacred Scripture, but this opinion was not allowed to go unchallenged by a number of the most influential among them. Origen (185-254), for example, accepted 'the Apocrypha' as a churchman, but as a scholar he limited the Old Testament Scriptures to the books of the Hebrew Canon. Cyril of Jerusalem (d. 386) taught his catechumens on the basis of the Hebrew Canon, but accepted the common use of the other writings. Jerome (d. 420) pronounced as his considered judgment that only the books of the Hebrew Canon should be considered authoritative and so canonical. He distinguished between what he called the *libri canonici* and the *libri ecclesiastici*. These latter, which were outside the Hebrew Canon, should be placed '*inter apocrypha*', among the apocryphal writings, an expression which had been used already (apparently for the first time) by Cyril of Jerusalem. In practice, however, Jerome included the books of 'the Apocrypha' in his Latin translation which came to be known as the Vulgate, the official Roman Catholic version of the Scriptures. On the basis of the Vulgate the Roman Catholic Church pronounced 'the Apocrypha' canonical by the Council of Trent in 1546 and by the Vatican Council in 1870.

The attitude of the Reformers to 'the Apocrypha' was largely determined by the use which had for long been made of these writings by the Roman Catholic Church in support of such doctrines as salvation by works, the merits of the saints, Purgatory and intercession for the dead. This, together with a revival of interest in the Hebrew language, set the books of the Hebrew Canon in a class apart. Martin Luther (1534) segregated 'the Apocrypha' (apart from I and II Esdras) from the Hebrew Canon and placed them in an appendix to his Old Testament, describing them as 'books which cannot be reckoned with the canonical books and yet are useful and good for reading'. Coverdale (1535) also appended 'the Apocrypha' to his Old Testament, omitting the Prayer of Manasses (later included in the 'Great Bible', 1539) and adding I and II Esdras. 'The Apocrypha', either in the body of the Old Testament or as an appendix, thereafter appeared in 'Matthew's Bible' (1537), the Great Bible (1539), the Geneva Bible (1560), the Bishop's Bible (1568) and the Authorized Version of James I (1611). But the old controversy continued and as early as 1629 'the Apocrypha' was omitted from some editions of the English Bible and, from 1827, from the editions of the British and Foreign Bible Society, with the exception of some pulpit Bibles. Today, in Protestant eyes, the value of 'the Apocrypha' ranges from 'edifying' to 'of no religious value'.

Part Two

THE APOCALYPTISTS

5

The Message and Method of Apocalyptic

BROADLY speaking, the Jewish apocalyptic literature comes between the literature of the Old Testament and that of the New Testament and is closely linked up with both. On the one hand, it is a continuation of the Old Testament, for in many of its features it is a development of Hebrew prophecy. On the other hand, it is an anticipation of the New Testament, for it marks an important period of transition in which beliefs, emerging in these writings, were taken up and developed within the setting of Christianity; indeed, the important changes in religious thinking which took place in the period between the Testaments would, to a considerable extent, be unexplained and inexplicable were it not for the fact that we possess this body of Jewish literature. This applies particularly to the idea of the Messiah in his relation to the Son of Man and to the belief in the life after death. These two concepts will be dealt with in the final two chapters of this book and will indicate the significant contribution made by the apocalyptists to the development of religious beliefs during the inter-testamental period.

For some time these apocalyptic writings continued to be popular among the Christians. The pattern of Jewish apocalyptic is evident within the New Testament Canon, particularly in the Apocalypse of John and in the so-called Little Apocalypse of Mark 13; but quite apart from these, many other apocalypses were written in imitation of the earlier Jewish books. This is not really surprising, for the message of the Jewish apocalyptic writers was very much in line with Christian hopes and expectations. It pointed men away from this evil and troubled world to the great unfolding purpose of Almighty God who held the history and the destiny of the world in the hollow of his hand. The day was fast approaching when he would intervene in power and establish his kingdom of righteousness and peace; the Messianic Age, soon to dawn, would bring with it the blessings of Paradise; the great Day of Judgment would witness the overthrow of the wicked and the vindication of the righteous; the New Age was just around the corner, the Kingdom of God was at hand! It is not at all surprising, then, that such teaching should be greatly prized within the Christian Church, for it was surely a foretelling of the triumph of that same kingdom in which the Christians themselves believed. Only when the Christian expectation of an early return of Christ faded did these books and their Christian counterparts fall out of favour, although again and again in the course of its history the Church has turned for inspiration and encouragement to the message which the apocalyptists proclaimed.

It is possible to trace patterns and schemes in these writers' thoughts, but the reader must not expect to find measured consistency or logical presentation in the ideas and beliefs expressed in this literature. As Dr F. C. Burkitt remarks, 'The chief danger now is that too strict a standard of consistency and rationality may be exacted from writers to whom consistency and rationality were quite secondary considerations. Consistency and rationality belong to the past, and to the course of events in this world: the apocalyptist's part is to stimulate his comrades by sketches of the future. And a future in which everything is consistent . . . the heart of man has not conceived.'[1]

I. THE APOCALYPTIC TRADITION

The Jewish apocalyptic literature, which flourished from 165 B.C. to A.D. 90, owes much to the preparation of the Old Testament prophets and to the influence of foreign ideas, especially those connected with the Zoroastrian eschatology of the Persian Empire. But it is true to say that it took root in the time of persecution under Antiochus IV (Epiphanes) and thrived in the atmosphere of oppression, torture and threat of death which prevailed in Palestine throughout that monarch's reign. The seed had already been sown, as it were, in such passages as Ezekiel 38-39, Zechariah 9-14, certain parts of Joel, and Isaiah 24-27 which, interestingly enough, are themselves embedded in prophecy; but in the events leading up to the Maccabean Revolt this seed was brought to full flower. The first, and undoubtedly the greatest, of these apocalyptic writings is the Book of Daniel, written against a background of persecution, terror and death. From the very beginning it must have won an honoured place among those for whom it was written and have made a very deep impression on the Jewish people as a whole; it alone of all those that followed ultimately won for itself a place within the Canon of the Hebrew Scriptures.

A. *The hidden secret*

Throughout practically the whole of this literature a set pattern can be traced which, though it varies in detail, is almost always the same in broad outline. The several writings claim to be revelations of divine secrets which God made known to certain elect individuals (ranging from Adam to Ezra) who purport to be

[1] *Jewish and Christian Apocalypses*, 1914, p. 48.

the writers of the books. These men, by visions and the like, had been initiated into an understanding of the secrets of heaven and subsequently recorded them in their 'hidden' books as instruction for the righteous. The nature of this initiation varies in different parts of the literature. Frequently it takes the form of a translation either in the spirit[1] or in the body[2] into heaven itself. There the ancient seer is admitted into the eternal secrets of the divine purpose or even into the very presence of God.[3]

In several of the apocalyptic writings reference is made to 'heavenly tablets' on which are recorded the secrets of the ages. In I Enoch they record 'all the deeds of mankind . . . to the remotest generations' (81.2, cf. 93.2) and foretell the unrighteousness which will appear on the earth (106.19; 107.1). Elsewhere they are called 'the books of the holy ones'; in them the angels learn of the future and so are able to prepare for the recompense of the righteous and the wicked (cf. 103.2; 106.19; 108.7). This same idea is present in the Book of Jubilees (cf. 1.29; 5.13; 23.30-32; 30.21-22, etc.) and in the Testaments of the Twelve Patriarchs where the heavenly tablets are believed to predict future events (cf. Test. of Asher 7.5) and stress is laid on the

[1] Cf. I Enoch 71.1. The words, 'Come up hither', in Rev. 11.12, spoken to John on the isle of Patmos probably refer to a translation of the spirit. Cf. also Rev. 17.3; 21.10.

[2] Cf. I Enoch 39.3, 4; II Enoch 3.1; 36.1, 2; 38.1; Test. of Abraham 7B, 8B; Apoc. of Baruch 6.3; II Esdras 14.9. We are reminded of the words of Paul in II Cor. 12.2-4 where he tells how he was caught up to the third heaven 'whether in the body, I know not; or whether out of the body, I know not'.

[3] Cf. I Enoch 14.9-17; 71.7-9; II Enoch 20.3; 22.1, etc. There are many legendary stories, especially in Greek literature, of a man's soul travelling through Hades or Heaven either after death or in a state of trance. The apocalyptists, however, were probably more deeply influenced by the Old Testament idea of a Heavenly Council presided over by God and attended by angels and sometimes men. Cf. I Kings 22.19ff; Job 1.6ff; Isa. 6.6ff; Ps. 89.7; Jer. 23.18ff. This same idea is developed to an extravagant degree in later Judaism (cf. *Sanhedrin* xxxviii. 6).

determinism of future events[1] (cf. Test. of Asher 2.10; Test. of Levi 5.4).

Such secrets, though having a particular bearing on 'the last things', relate to the whole purpose of God for the universe from the creation to the end-time. An understanding of such secrets helps the righteous to discern the signs of the approaching end and establishes them in their holy faith.[2] Quite often the revelation vouchsafed to the ancient worthy consists of an account of world history culminating in the Messianic Kingdom or the Age to Come. Generally speaking the account given is fairly clear, beneath its symbolic devices, right up to the age in which the author himself is actually living; and then, inevitably, the account becomes obscure, for although the whole account purports to be prediction in the name of the ancient seer, prediction proper actually begins at the point of the author's own day. From this point onwards the tempo of events is greatly quickened, for the end is at hand. The nature of the end and the details of its coming show a great diversity of thought, but usually the writer depicts the overthrow of the wicked and the triumph of the righteous, either in this world or in the life to come, in an earthly kingdom or in a heavenly, in their physical bodies or in renewed 'spiritual' bodies; the Messianic Kingdom, temporal or eternal, is ushered in and heralds or inaugurates the Age to Come when God's purposes will triumph and he will live with his people for evermore.[3] This pattern of revelation tended to become stereotyped and formal, but in its origins at any rate, as in the Book of Daniel, its purpose was a very practical one, namely, to inspire the nation with a new courage and with fresh hope in the ultimate victory of good over evil and in

[1] For the place of determinism in the apocalyptists' interpretation of history see p. 106.
[2] For the revealing of the divine secret by the Son of Man, see pp. 134, 140.
[3] See further pp. 145ff, 149ff.

the triumph of God and his kingdom over all the powers of darkness.

B. *The language of symbolism*

The whole of this literature abounds in imagery of a fantastic and bizarre kind, to such an extent that symbolism may be said to be the language of apocalyptic. Some of this symbolism is taken over directly from the Old Testament whose imagery and metaphors are adapted and used as material for figurative representation. Much of it, however, has its origin in ancient mythology. This influence is traceable even in the Old Testament itself, but in apocalyptic it is much more fully developed. Some of the pictures and allusions no doubt originated with the apocalyptic writers themselves under the influence of foreign ideas and became part of their common stock.

Of particular interest is the ancient Babylonian myth of a combat between the divine Creator and a great sea monster. This myth finds echoes in a number of passages in the Old Testament where the monster is variously described as the Dragon, Leviathan, Rahab or the Serpent.[1] In Babylonian and Hebrew forms alike it symbolizes the chaotic deep or cosmic ocean (Hebrew *Tehôm*, Babylonian *Tiâmat*)[2] which is regarded as a place of mystery and evil. Elsewhere it is identified with Egypt (cf. Ps 87.4) which in several places is described under the figure of great sea monster (cf. Ps. 74.13ff; Ezek. 29.3; 32.2).

This same monster reappears in apocalyptic in several writings of various dates. In the Testament of Asher, for example, the writer tells of the coming of the Most High to earth and of his

[1] Dragon (Job 7.12; Ps. 74.13; Isa. 51.9; Ezek. 29.3; 32.2), Leviathan (Job 41.1; Ps. 74.14; 104.26; Isa. 27.1), Rahab (Job 9.13; 26.12; Ps. 89.10; Isa.30.7; 51.9), Serpent (Job 26.13; Isa. 27.1; Amos 9.3).
[2] Cf. Job 7.12; 26.12; 38.8; Ps. 74.13; Isa. 51.10; Hab. 3.8; Amos 7.. For the power of God over the deep see also Ps. 33.7f; 93.1ff; 107.23-32; Jonah 2.5-9, etc. In Gen. 1.2, 6ff, God the Creator saves the world from the power of chaos in the form of the primeval ocean.

'breaking the head of the dragon in the water' (7.3, cf. Ps. 74.13). There is a tradition that this dragon, described as Behemoth and Leviathan, is to be devoured at the Messianic Banquet by those who remain in the Messianic Age (II Esdras 6.52; II Baruch 29.4).[1] In the Zadokite Fragments the same figure is used to describe 'the kings of the Gentiles' (9.19-20), whilst in the Psalms of Solomon the reference is to the Roman general Pompey (2.29), no doubt under the influence of Jeremiah 51.34, where Nebuchadnezzar of Babylon is referred to in similar terms.

Throughout the apocalyptic literature great use is made of animal figures of all kinds to symbolize men and nations. The figure of the bull, for example, already familiar in the Old Testament as a symbol of God's presence and power,[2] appears particularly in I Enoch 85-86 as a symbol of the patriarchs from Adam to Isaac. In one passage it represents the human Messiah and the members of his kingdom who become white bulls just like Adam (I Enoch 90.37-38). The righteous who come after the patriarchs are described under the figures of sheep or lambs, no doubt under the influence of Ezek. 34.3, 6, 8, where the same symbolism is used.[3] Moses and Aaron and many others after them are referred to in this way (I Enoch 89.16, 18). David and Solomon, for example, are sheep until they come to the throne and then they become rams (I Enoch 89.45, 48). The Messiah, as we have seen, is a white bull but, on entering his kingdom, he becomes a lamb (I Enoch 90.38). Judas Maccabaeus is described as a ram (90.14) and elsewhere as a great horn (90.9). The ram is, of course, a well-known symbol of might and dominion (cf.

---

[1] In the Book of Revelation the Dragon appears as Satan and is the enemy of the Messiah and his saints (cf. 12.9, 20.2). Reference is made to the Messianic Banquet in rabbinic literature; among the literature from Qumran the 'Rule of the Congregation' describes certain arrangements for a banquet which is presumably set in the new age (see p. 129).

[2] Cf. Ex. 32.4ff; I Kings 12.26ff; Hos. 10.5, etc.

[3] Cf. also Ps. 74.1; 79.13; 100.3; Jer. 23.1, where Israel is the sheep of God's pasture.

Ezek. 34.17; 39.18) and is found also in other apocalyptic writings (cf. Dan. 8.3f, etc.).

Frequent use is made by the apocalyptists of wild beasts and birds of prey to symbolize the nations of the Gentiles. No doubt they were influenced in this by such a passage as Ezek. 39.17ff and perhaps too by the Book of Job and the Book of Proverbs where great interest is shown in nature and frequent references are made to animal figures of many kinds. The most extensive list is found in I Enoch 89.10ff where the various Gentile nations are described under the figures of lions, tigers, wolves, dogs, hyenas, wild boars, foxes, squirrels, swine, falcons, vultures, kites, eagles and ravens. In the Testament of Joseph 19.8, however, the lion is used to represent Judah, and in II Esdras 11.37 it symbolizes the Messiah.[1] In this latter case the lion, speaking with the voice of a man, upbraids and then destroys 'the eagle' (11.37ff) which, as the author tells us (12.11), represents the fourth kingdom in the vision of Daniel (Dan. 7.23), which is here identified with Rome. In Daniel's vision there come up out of the sea four great beasts belonging to no recognizable species. The first is like a lion with eagles' wings (7.4); the second is like a bear, having three ribs in its mouth (v.5); the third is like a leopard with four wings (v.6); the fourth is a beast with ten horns and great iron teeth (v.7). By means of this strange symbolism, whose roots go far back into ancient mythology, the author depicts the four great Empires of Babylonia, Media, Persia and Greece.

Just as men and nations are symbolized by animals, so good angels are symbolized by men[2] and fallen angels by stars.[3] This latter usage is found particularly in I Enoch 85-90, where Enoch,

[1] Cf. Rev. 5.5 where the Messiah is called 'the Lion of the tribe of Judah'.

[2] Cf. I Enoch 87.2ff; 89.59; 90.21; Test. of Levi 8.2; II Enoch 1.4, etc. For a somewhat similar usage in the Old Testament see Gen. 18.2ff; Ezek. 9.2, etc.

[3] Cf. Rev. 1.20 where this language is used to describe 'the angels of the seven churches'.

in a vision, sees a star, representing Azazel the prince of the fallen angels, falling from heaven followed by many other stars, representing all his host (86.1ff). Another version of this story tells how the fallen angels cohabit with the daughters of men who produce a monstrous race of giants (I Enoch 7.1ff; 15.1ff; 86.1ff).[1] These giants are destroyed by the Flood, but their spirits are let loose as demons to corrupt all mankind (15.8ff). The fallen angels, called 'Watchers' (the name is used for the first time in Dan. 4.13, 17, 23), are to be punished even before the Final Judgment, but the punishment of the demons will be reserved until that great Day (cf. I Enoch 10.6; 16.1; 19.1).[2]

Another form of symbolism to be found in the apocalyptic writings is that of number, especially the numbers 3, 4, 7, 10 and 12 or multiples of them.[3] Each of these has a peculiar religious significance in the Old Testament and at least some of them appear fairly frequently in Babylonian and Persian sources. A special importance attaches to the number 7, denoting completion or perfection, which appears in apocalyptic writings throughout the whole of the inter-testamental period in passages too numerous to mention.[4]

c. *The Ezra-legend*

Interesting light is thrown on the tradition of this apocalyptic literature by the so-called Ezra-legend contained in chapter 14 of II Esdras, but no doubt excerpted from an independent source. It tells how, as Ezra sat under an oak tree, he heard a voice calling him out of a bush bidding him lay up in his heart the signs which God would show him, just as Moses had done in days gone by;

[1] Cf. Gen. 6.1ff for a biblical account of this old myth in which evil is traced to the fallen angels.
[2] This belief is expressed also in Jubilees 10.5-11 and is hinted at in Matt. 8.29, 'Art thou come hither to torment us before the time?'
[3] See further pp. 106ff, 137.
[4] The popularity of the number 7 is obvious in the Book of Revelation, where it occurs 54 times.

the present world order was fast drawing to a close and he must soon ascend to be with the Messiah. Thereupon he is bidden to set aside forty days in which, under divine inspiration, he would dictate to five chosen companions 'all that has happened in the world since the beginning, even the things which were written in thy law'. Ezra did as he was commanded and in forty days dictated to the five men ninety-four books.[1] This injunction then came from the Almighty, 'The twenty-four books that thou hast written publish that the worthy and unworthy may read (therein); but the seventy last thou shalt keep, to deliver them to the wise among thy people' (14.45-46).

This account is a re-application of the familiar tradition that Ezra was the restorer of the Law of Moses which, it was believed, had been burned (14.21) when Jerusalem was destroyed by Nebuchadnezzar. On Mount Sinai Moses had received a divine revelation in which God 'told him many wondrous things, showed him the secrets of the times, declared to him the end of the seasons' (14.5). The words of the Law he had to publish openly, but the secret tradition concerning the crisis of world history he had to keep to himself (14.6). It seems obvious that the writer has in mind here the apocalyptic tradition believed to have been received from Moses together with the sacred Law and now restored by Ezra under the inspiration of God. The twenty-four books which were to be published openly were the books of canonical Scripture, and the seventy which were to be kept secret and delivered only to the wise were the esoteric apocalyptic writings. The number seventy is no doubt used symbolically to signify a comprehensive figure and is probably meant to include not only those apocalyptic books, known and unknown, which appeared under the name of Moses, but also the wider range of

[1] Cf. II Enoch 23.3f where Enoch writes 366 books at the dictation of the archangel Vretil, and the Assumption of Moses 1.16; 10.11; 11.1 where Moses is bidden to preserve the heavenly books which God would deliver to him.

apocalyptic writings including this book itself in which these events are recorded.

This Ezra-legend, then, claims in effect for the apocalyptic tradition a valued and authoritative place within Judaism. It no doubt reflects the conscientious belief in certain apocalyptic circles at that time that this type of literature, like the Oral Tradition itself (cf. Pirke Aboth 1.1), could be traced back to its source in the revelation given by God to Moses on Mount Sinai. It had been suggested that 'in Ezra and his five companions there may be a covert allusion to the great Rabbi Johanan b. Zakkai—the re-founder of Judaism after A.D. 66-70—and his five famous disciples'.[1] If this be so it strengthens still further the argument that the author is here claiming for the apocalyptic tradition an essential place in the life of reformed Judaism.

2. APOCALYPTIC AND PROPHECY

The apocalyptic writers believed that they stood in the true prophetic tradition of the Old Testament Scriptures and were convinced that, like the prophets of old, they too had a message from God.[2] In particular they were concerned with the predictive element which they found in prophecy and which had been largely neglected in the rabbinic methods of their day. Their method was to fasten on predictions made in the past which had not been fulfilled in the literal sense of the passages concerned and to see in them hidden and symbolic meanings which they would proceed to recast and re-interpret. By thus re-interpreting and re-applying the message of prophecy to succeeding generations they showed it to be not only a 'forth-telling' but a 'fore-telling' of

---

[1] G. H. Box, *The Ezra-Apocalypse*, 1912, p. 314.
[2] The Rabbis also made this claim for themselves. In the Talmud the following words are put into the mouth of a Rabbi of the third century A.D., 'Prophecy was taken from the Prophets and was given to the wise, and it has not been taken from these' (*Baba Bathra* 12a).

the word of God. For this reason apocalyptic has sometimes been described as 'unfulfilled prophecy', and to a large extent this is true. An example of this is to be found in Jeremiah's prediction of seventy years' captivity before the final restoration (Jer. 25.11; 29.10) which is interpreted by the writer of Daniel as seventy weeks of years (9.24), and by the writer of I Enoch as the seventy reigns of the seventy 'shepherds' or angels commissioned by God to shepherd his people Israel (89.59ff). Another example is the prophecy recorded in Dan. 7.23. There the fourth beast obviously represents Greece,[1] but in II Esdras 12.11 it is given an entirely new interpretation and now represents Rome.[2]

The form which the apocalyptists' message assumed was in many respects different from that of the prophets; nevertheless it was a true continuation and development of the prophetic message and in several respects brought it to its logical conclusion. This can be illustrated by reference to three aspects of their message—their conception of the unity of history, their eschatological ideas and their belief concerning the form of divine inspiration.

A. *The unity of history*

Dr R. H. Charles maintains that it was 'apocalyptic and not prophecy that was the first to grasp the great idea that all history, human, cosmological and spiritual is a unity', that 'Daniel was the first to teach the unity of all human history, and that every fresh phase of this history was a further stage in the development of God's purpose'.[3] But Dr Charles, in writing thus, is not quite fair to the prophets in the zeal he has for the apocalyptists. The belief in monotheism and the belief in the all-embracing purpose of God are correlatives and these are to be found implicitly in

[1] See p. 100.
[2] A similar interpretation is given of Dan. 7.23 in the Babylonian Talmud, '*Aboda Zara* 1b.
[3] *Commentary on Daniel*, 1929, pp. xxv, cxiv-cxv.

Amos and explicitly in Deutero-Isaiah. The glance of these prophets sweeps indiscriminately over past, present and future, uniting all history into a single plan, conceived and controlled by God. It may be true, as Dr Charles says, that 'whereas prophecy incidentally dealt with the past and devoted itself to the present and the future as rising organically out of the past, apocalyptic, though its interests lie chiefly in the future as containing the solution of the problems of the past and the present, took within its purview things past, present and to come'.[1] This does not necessarily imply, however, that the prophets did not thereby grasp the idea of the unity of history; indeed the evidence of their writings implies that they did. But if the prophets were the first to grasp this idea, it was left to the apocalyptists to complete the logic of it.

Following the lead of the prophets, the apocalyptists set about relating the data of history to one another and traced the connection between them in the divine purpose underlying history. They saw and interpreted the events of history *sub specie aeternitatis*, observing in its apparent confusion an order and a goal. 'The apocalyptists believed in God, and believed that He had some purpose for the world He had made, and that His power was equal to its achievement. Their faith goes beyond the faith in the divine control of history, indeed. It is a faith in the divine initiative in history for the attainment of its final goal.'[2]

The advance of the apocalyptists on the prophets in this respect is to be seen in two directions: they began to work out history in vast periods not only systematically but deterministically. There was known among them a secret tradition concerning the crises of world history associated with the name of Moses which takes different forms in different writings. In the Assumption of Moses 10.12 the writer describes Moses as saying, 'From my death until

[1] *Eschatology*, 1913, p. 183.
[2] H. H. Rowley, *The Relevance of Apocalyptic*, 1944, p. 142.

his advent there shall be CCL times', i.e. 250 year-weeks or 1,750 years which, when added to the 2,500 years which had elapsed before the death of Moses, makes the duration of world history 85 Jubilees or 4,250 years. This scheme of history is systematized still more in the Apocalpyse of Weeks (I Enoch 93.1-10; 91.12-17) where it is divided into ten 'weeks' of unequal length,[1] each marked by some great event. From the standpoint of the writer the first seven weeks are in the past and the last three weeks are in the future, the Messianic Kingdom being set up in the eighth week and continuing till the close of the tenth week when the Final Judgment takes place. In other writings the division is made into seven parts (Test. of Abraham 17, 19) or into twelve parts (Apoc. of Abraham 20, 28; II Esdras 14.11; 2 Baruch 53.6; 56.3). These systematically arranged divisions of time form a unity of history in and through which can be traced the unfailing purpose of God. The present age is brought to its close in the Final Judgment or in the establishment of the Messianic Kingdom.

Not only did the apocalyptists divide up history into different periods of time; history, thus conceived, had been determined beforehand by the will of God and revealed to his servants. God had set down on the heavenly tablets[2] the fixed order of events from which there could be no deviation whatsoever. 'That which is determined shall be done' (Dan. 11.36). He had determined beforehand the destinies of Israel and the nations (Ass. of Moses 12.4f) and recorded all the deeds of mankind (Jubilees 1.29); he would bring this present age to a close when the predetermined time was fulfilled (II Esdras 4.36; 11.44). Men could not alter what was predetermined by God, but they could at least investigate the scheme of history and try to discover at what point in it

[1] Cf. The Sibylline Oracles Book IV, lines 47ff, where world history is also divided into ten 'generations'.
[2] See pp. 96f.

they themselves stood by identifying past historical events with specific events in the scheme. The calculation of times, therefore, became a very important part of the apocalyptists' job and led them almost always to the conclusion that they were standing in the last days. Behind everything, from the very beginning to the very end, lay the predetermined purpose of God binding the whole of history into one.

Two factors helped the apocalyptists to widen and develop their conception of the unity of history. One was the external influence of Zoroastrianism;[1] the other was the internal influence of beliefs and conditions within Judaism and within the Jewish state.

Characteristic of Zoroastrian teaching was the idea that the world would last for a period of 12,000 years, consisting of four eras of 3,000 years each. During the first of these everything is invisible;[2] during the second the great god Ahura-Mazda creates the material world and man; during the third Angra-Mainyu, the great evil spirit, has power over men; during the fourth men gradually approach a state of perfection through the work of Shaoshyant the saviour. The Iranian writers, that is, divide up history into great world epochs and work out elaborate schemes and systems of measurement much in the same way as the Jewish apocalyptists. There can be no doubt that these apocalyptists were greatly influenced by Iranian thought in this particular respect. It cannot be without significance, for example, that the number 12 which plays such an important part in Zoroastrianism should appear so frequently in the Jewish divisions of history. The Jewish apocalyptic writers, then, took over this Iranian conception of great world epochs and used it to make more vivid and more wide-embracing the idea which they had received from

[1] See pp. 21ff.
[2] Cf. II Enoch 24.4, 'For before all things were visible, I alone used to go about in the invisible things'.

the prophets of a unity of history brought about by the unfailing purpose of Almighty God.

The second factor influencing these writers was the nature of the prevailing beliefs and conditions within Palestine. From the time of the Maccabean Revolt in 167 B.C. down to the destruction of the Temple in A.D. 70 the Jewish people had been welded together into a nation, in many respects very much like other small nations around Palestine. But they were much more conscious of the differences between themselves and others than they were of any similarities. The Jewish nation could not be compared in material power with the great Empires of the Seleucids and Ptolemies; nevertheless it believed that it had an imperial part to play in the history of civilization. This is the impression conveyed by the Book of Daniel, for example, as it contemplates the fulfilment of God's purpose in and through his people, the Jews. Here 'the great Gentile kingdoms, like the Greek supremacy of the Seleucids and Ptolemies which seemed so overwhelming and terrible, are shown as phases in a world process whose end is the Kingdom of God'.[1] In the visions recorded in chapters 2, 7 and 8 the writer sees the fall of the great Empires of Babylon, Media, Persia and Greece. No longer, as in Jeremiah and Ezekiel, are the pronouncements of divine judgment given piecemeal; here in Daniel we have, in the words of Dr F. C. Burkitt, 'a philosophy of universal History'.[2] The Jewish nation, small though it is, sees itself against the back-cloth of these mighty powers; its outlook has become truly cosmopolitan. It is not inferior to the great nations; rather it is superior, for they must perish, but Israel will inherit the kingdom prepared by God. This panorama of world events, in which their nation was to play such a vital part, made possible for the apocalyptists a much wider view of the unity of history than had been possible for the prophets before them.

The divine purpose which ran through all history would not,

however, cease with the climax of history, for 'the Most High has made not one Age but two' (II Esdras 7.[50]). The Cosmos cannot be reduced to a harmonious whole; there is a marked contrast between this present age of ungodliness and the future age of righteousness.[1] Nevertheless, there is a link between the temporal and the eternal orders which cannot be broken; it is the purpose of God which binds the two together and which will at last be vindicated in the vindication of his people. And so the apocalyptists' study of history passes over into eschatology; the purpose of God, which finds its actualization in history, must seek its justification beyond history.

B. *The last things*

Dr R. H. Charles does right in pointing out that prophecy and apocalyptic each has its own doctrine of 'the last things', and in emphasizing the difference between them;[2] but it should also be remembered that the broad lines of prophetic eschatology were taken over by the apocalyptists and remained an essential part of their teaching, despite the modifications and developments through which that teaching went. As we shall see in a later chapter,[3] the idea prevailed in certain apocalyptic circles of a kingdom belonging to this world in which the Jews would triumph and the Gentiles would be overthrown. This hope in the restoration of Israel was in line with much prophetic teaching in the Old Testament.[4] Elsewhere, however, the influence of Persian thought was deeply felt with its dualistic view of the world and its transcendent view of the Messiah.[5] But even here the apocalyptists were conscious of their place in the prophetic tradition, for

[1] Cf. Apoc. of Abraham 29, 31, 32. This dualism probably owes much to the influence of Zoroastrianism. See p. 21.
[2] *Op. cit.*, pp. 177ff.   [3] See chapter 6.
[4] Cf. Zeph. 3.8-13; Nahum 1-3; Isa. 13.1ff; 52.3ff; Mal. 3.2ff; Joel 3.1ff, 12ff; Zech. 14.1ff, etc.
[5] See pp. 21f and 130ff.

they continued to read the ancient prophets in the light of the future hope and to interpret their prophecies in terms of their new eschatological expectations.

The apocalyptists' belief in the life after death went far beyond anything to be found in the prophets and was no doubt again influenced by Persian thought. But even this belief was built up on the prophetic hope of restoration—not for the nation only, in an earthly kingdom, but for the individual also, in a heavenly kingdom.[1]

Of particular interest in this connection is the apocalyptic conception of the Day of Final Judgment which may be described as a specialization of the prophetic Day of the Lord. H. Wheeler Robinson sees in this prophetic 'Day' four characteristics—judgment, universality, supernatural intervention and proximity. In addition he notes four features contained in it—it brings to a focus the manifestation of God's purpose in history; it is a day on which God acts and not merely speaks; it is a day on which God is shown to be victorious within this present world-order and on the stage of human history; it is a day which ushers in a new era on the earth.[2]

It is of interest to observe that all these characteristics and features can be traced in the apocalyptic Day of Final Judgment. There are differences, it is true, some of which may have been caused by foreign influence; but in the vast majority of cases these differences appear as developments within the prophetic idea. For example, the emphasis came increasingly to be laid not so much on God's judgment within time and on the plane of history, as on his judgment in a setting beyond time and above history; the idea of judgment was no longer confined to the living but was extended to include the dead; instead of taking the form of a great crisis or great crises in history determining the fate of

---

[1] For a fuller treatment of this subject see chapter 7.
[2] Cf. *Inspiration and Revelation in the Old Testament*, 1946, pp. 137ff.

nations, the Final Judgment tended to assume a definitely forensic character in which individual men were judged.[1] Influenced though they were, then, by ideas foreign to the Hebrew tradition, the apocalyptists did not lose sight of the prophetic teaching concerning the future hope, but enlarged it and enriched it out of their own religious insight and experience.

c. *The form of inspiration*

It has sometimes been suggested that apocalyptic is simply imitative of prophecy and that it is an attempt to fulfil the word of Scripture by a means which has no relation to the present because it arises out of literary reflection. Certainly it is difficult to determine to what extent theirs was a genuine experience of inspiration and to what extent it was a conventional inspiration of a literary type. But the apocalyptists were not mere plagiarists, stiltedly copying and reproducing what the prophets had spoken. They were deeply religious men who believed that, like the prophets before them, their message was from God and that they wrote under a divine compulsion.

Like the prophets, the apocalyptists shared the popular belief in the accessibility of man's nature to the invasive Spirit of God and developed this belief to include the invasive spirits of evil which, like the Spirit of God, could take possession of a man and exercise control. In all probability descriptions of inspiration in which a man became 'possessed' had become, to a fairly large extent, a stereotyped convention in this type of literature; but it may be that in the apocalyptic books this description reflects a personal experience of the writer himself. In II Esdras 14 an attempt is made to rationalize previous ideas of inspiration which represented man's nature as open to incursions of the invasive Spirit of God and in which spirit is thought of (as in pre-exilic times) in a very material way. There the prophet is bidden to

[1] See pp. 153ff.

drink from a cup 'full as it were with water, but the colour of it was like fire' (14.39). It is the cup of inspiration filled with the holy spirit by which he is able to dictate aloud the twenty-four books of Scripture and the seventy apocalyptic writings. Unlike the ecstatic prophets of the Old Testament Ezra finds that his faculties are strengthened rather than weakened and in particular his mind is clarified so that he can remember perfectly the sacred writings.

Many references are made in this literature to demon possession. Indeed, demonology here comes into its own, and evil spirits are said to be sent forth to invade the lives of men (cf. Test. of Dan 1.7, Test. of Zebulun 2.1; 3.2, Martyrdom of Isaiah 3.11, etc.). This personalization of malignant powers, encouraged no doubt by Persian influence, reflects the beliefs of the writers concerned and affirms their own awareness of the reality of invasive powers both of good and evil.

Frequent mention is made in these writings of such media as dreams, visions, trances and auditions by whose means God conveys his revelation to the ancient worthy in whose name the author writes. In the vast majority of cases it is quite impossible to say when the portrayed abnormal experience is anything more than a mere literary device or convention. What Dr Charles says is no doubt true. 'Just as at times the prophet came to use the words, "Thus saith the Lord", even when there was no actual psychical experience in which he heard a voice, but when he wished to set forth the will of God which he had reached by other means, so the term "vision" came to have a like conventional use both in prophecy and apocalyptic.'[1] At the same time, however, it must not be overlooked that inspiration can take hold of the conventional and the cliché. There is no guarantee that the inspired message will be passed on in its original forms. The fact that the prophets, for example, make use of a common conven-

---

[1] *Op. cit.*, p. 176.

tional form, namely rhythmical versification, does not in any way affect the ultimate inspiration; and to say that the apocalyptists, in their utterances, make use of some form of literary convention does not necessarily imply that they are any less inspired for so doing. Much of this literary convention may well have psychological experience behind it.

Indeed many of the experiences recorded here concerning the supposed writer of the book are so true psychologically that it is difficult to see in them nothing more than the expression of literary convention. In receiving the divine revelation he lies on the ground as one dead (II Esdras 10.30; cf. Dan. 8.17f, etc.), he is so overwhelmed that he cannot describe it adequately (II Esdras 10.32, 55f; cf. II Cor. 12.4), he is not only alarmed in his thoughts (Dan. 7.28) but is even physically sick (Dan. 8.27) and loses consciousness altogether (Dan. 8.18); sometimes he is even insensible to all physical suffering as when his body is sawn asunder (Martyrdom of Isaiah 5.7). In these examples and many more we are tempted to see a projection of the apocalyptist's own psychical experience. This is how the writer thought inspiration could come, and so there is at least an *a priori* argument for the possibility of his sharing such an experience. He ascribes to the one in whose name he writes such experiences as he would expect to have in a message to himself, and some of these may well have been genuine experiences in which he believed himself to be divinely inspired.

Perhaps it is a true evaluation to say that in apocalyptic inspiration we have a link between the original inspiration of the prophets and the more modern inspiration of a literary kind. Again and again the apocalyptist shows that he believed himself to be writing under the direct influence of the Spirit of God in a manner akin to that of the prophets, and even when he accepted the conventional literary frame-work, as often he did, he still believed himself to be divinely inspired.

3. PSEUDONYMITY

In one important respect the apocalyptists differed from the prophets in whose tradition they followed. The prophets spoke from the point of view of their own day and, under God, uttered their oracles in their own name; the apocalyptists wrote from the point of view of a previous age and, still under God, penned their oracles in the name of another. Generally speaking it is true to say that apocalyptic is pseudonymous. The authors wrote in the name of some notable man of the past to whom was given a revelation of the things to come; this revelation he was charged to seal up and keep secret until the time appointed. With the issuing of the book the hour had come for the secret to be revealed, for the End was at hand. This phenomenon of pseudonymity had already been long familiar to the Egyptians and was also known among the Greeks. But the particular form which it took in Palestine seems to indicate an indigenous development and an expression of native Hebrew thought.

A. *A literary device*

The familiar explanation of the origin of Jewish pseudonymity is that given by Dr R. H. Charles who maintains that, from the time of Ezra onwards, the Law claimed an all-sufficiency which left no room for fresh revelations of truth apart from itself. Inspiration was dead; the voice of prophecy was dumb. The apocalyptists believed, however, that they were recipients of fresh revelations from God. 'Against the reception of such fresh faith and truth, the Law stood in the way, unless the books containing them came under the aegis of certain great names in the past. Against the claims and authority of such names, the official representatives of the Law were in part reduced to silence.'[1] In support of this

[1] *Op. cit.*, p. 203.

view he points out that by about 200 B.C. the prophetic Canon was fixed and so no books of a prophetic character could thereafter be included. Moreover, as the Hagiographa (the third section within the Canon) grew and crystallized, a test of any book claiming admittance was that it should be as early as the time of Ezra when inspiration was deemed to have ceased. If, therefore, the apocalyptist was to obtain a hearing it was necessary for him to issue his book in the name of some person at least as early as the time of Ezra.

But, quite apart from the fact that the Law did not exercise the 'unquestioned autocracy' which Dr Charles claims for it, this explanation accuses the apocalyptists not only of deception, but of credulity in believing that such deception would be accepted by their readers at its face value. There is strong reason to believe, indeed, that the Jews were not particularly interested in authorship as such; nor is there evidence to show that their books would not have been read had they been issued simply anonymously or in their own names.

Another explanation has been put forward by Dr H. H. Rowley who says that 'the pseudonymity of the Book of Daniel grew out of its genesis, and that it was not consciously intended from the start, but that succeeding writers slavishly copied this feature, as though it were part of the technique of apocalyptic'.[1] The suggestion is that the stories of the first part of Daniel were issued as messages for the time, most of them centring in the figure of Daniel. The author of these stories, whose identity was not revealed, thereafter issued an account of his visions, and 'wrote them under the guise of Daniel, not in order to deceive his readers, but in order to reveal his identity with the author of the Daniel stories. Pseudonymity was thus born of a living process, whose purpose was the precise opposite of deceit. It only became artificial when it was woodenly copied by imitators.'

[1] *Op. cit.*, p. 36.

B. *Extension of personality*

It may well be that the adoption of a pseudonym on the part of some of these writers was in fact a literary device which was subsequently copied by others and that the genesis of pseudonymity may be traced back to the writing of the Book of Daniel in the way that H. H. Rowley describes. But in the case of certain of them at any rate there is perhaps reason to believe that its use indicates not simply a literary convention, but a genuine experience of inspiration.

This may be best explained by reference to the Hebrew conception of 'corporate personality' and in particular the idea of the 'extension of personality' which are without parallel in modern thought. According to the Hebrews a man's personality could be expressed in such things as 'the spoken and, no doubt, the written word, one's name, one's property and . . . one's offspring'.[1] Moreover, the group to which he belonged and in which his life was merged was not confined simply to its present members but was extended to include past and future members, the whole group forming a single unit. This whole group could 'function as a single individual through any one of these members conceived as representative of it'.[2]

Now the apocalyptists did not belong to a corporate group, but they did stand in a distinctive apocalyptic tradition which, many believed, could be traced back to Moses himself (cf. II Esdras 14.3ff). This tradition was represented not only by Moses but by men like Enoch and Ezra and Daniel who stood in the same line of succession. The apocalyptists believed themselves to be extensions of this tradition and representatives of it and so of their renowned predecessors in whose names they wrote. Just as a

[1] A. R. Johnson, *The Vitality of the Individual in the Thought of Ancient Israel*, 1949, p. 89.
[2] H. W. Robinson, 'The Hebrew Conception of Corporate Personality' in *Werden und Wesen des Alten Testaments* (BZAW, no. 66), 1936, p. 49.

portion of Elijah's spirit could come upon Elisha (II Kings 2.9) and the spirit which was upon Moses could be transferred to the seventy elders (Num. 11.16f), so the spirit of Moses or Enoch or Ezra or Daniel could speak through their later representatives.[1] If this be so, then the apocalyptists, in ascribing their writings to Moses and the rest, were not attempting to deceive their readers but were, in good faith, seeking to interpret to them what they believed to be the mind and message of the one in whose name and by whose inspiration they wrote.

c. *The significance of 'the name'*

Support for this view may be found in the very pseudonyms which the apocalyptists chose for themselves and in the importance which Hebrew thought attached to a person's name. To know a man's name was to know the very substance of his being; his character was involved in his name, and a change in the one might necessitate a change in the other. The name was essentially a social concept. It could be inherited and its substance depended very largely on the content already given to it by those from whom it had been received; normally its inheritance was confined to one's own family relations, but this was possible even outside these limits. In a word, the name represented an extension of a man's personality, particularly within the relationships of the group to which he belonged.

If it is possible to apply this reasoning to the problem of pseudonymity, then the apocalyptists, by appropriating the name of an ancient seer, were doing more than merely taking over an appellation; they were in effect associating themselves with him as an 'extension of his personality' within the apocalyptic tradition. But what evidence is there for such a claim? There are indications in several of the apocalyptic writings of a connection between the problems occupying the writer's mind and the

[1] Cf. H. W. Robinson, *Congregational Quarterly*, vol. xxii, no. 4, pp. 369f.

pseudonym which he chose; the subject to be treated and the writer's approach to it may well have suggested the name in which he was to reveal the divine secret.

The writer of the Book of Jubilees, for example, was concerned above all else with the glorification of the priesthood and the supremacy of the Law. It is not surprising, therefore, that the pseudonym under which he wrote was that of Moses whom the Scriptures describe not only as a law-giver but as a priest of God (cf. Ex. 24.6; 33.7ff; Ps. 99.6). Again, the outlook of the writers of I Enoch is largely cosmopolitan; there the history of mankind is described in the form of a vision; the heavenly bodies shine down on Jew and Gentile alike; the story is one of God's dealings with the whole human race. What better pseudonym could there be than that of Enoch? He was 'the great-great-grandfather of Shem, but he was the great-great-grandfather of Ham and Japhet too. What was Enoch's nationality? He might appropriately reply, Homo sum.'[1] Far removed from this cosmopolitan outlook is the narrow nationalistic outlook of II Esdras where the interest of the writer centres in Israel's part in the Messianic Kingdom and in the utter destruction of the Gentiles (cf. 13.38). The pseudonym of, say, Enoch would have been quite out of keeping in a book of this nature; it is appropriate that the author writes in the name of Ezra whose whole outlook was narrowly nationalistic and to whom the Gentiles were a contamination.

The adoption of pseudonymity was no doubt essentially a literary device, but this evidence, whilst not conclusive, may well indicate that behind this phenomenon lay an awareness of inspiration of a characteristically Hebrew kind understandable in terms of 'extension of personality' within the apocalyptic tradition. If this suggestion is correct, then it casts light on the reason for the esoteric nature of these writings and frees the apocalyptists from any charge of deception.

[1] F. C. Burkitt, op. cit., p. 19.

6

The Messiah and the Son of Man

IN both the Old Testament and the literature of the inter-testamental period much is said about the coming of a Golden Age, a 'Messianic Kingdom', in which the fortunes of Israel (or a remnant within Israel) would be restored, the surrounding nations judged and an era of justice and peace ushered in. But this phrase 'Messianic Kingdom' can be most misleading, for in both prophetic and apocalyptic writings, although the kingdom and the Messiah were often related, the figure of the Messiah is frequently absent. The Messiah and the messianic concept are not always or necessarily found together. It is true that those passages in the Old Testament which refer to the coming kingdom frequently refer also to an ideal leader at its head, but, apart from some references in the Psalms whose meaning is disputed, the passages do not use the term 'Messiah' to describe him. Conversely, in those passages where the term 'Messiah' is used, or in the great majority of them at any rate, the reference is not to the ideal figure at all, but to an actual historical person, usually the anointed king of Israel.

This fact reminds us that in the Old Testament the word 'Messiah' is not a technical expression signifying the name or title of the ideal leader of the future kingdom. It is simply an adjective, meaning 'anointed', descriptive of one who has been set apart by God for a special purpose. In two passages (I Kings 19.16; Ps. 105.15) the reference is to prophets, but the normal use of the word is in connection with kings.[1] When a man became king he was not crowned, but anointed with oil; he was thus set apart as a 'holy' man to a kingship possessing sacral and priestly functions. In post-exilic times, when the monarchy had ceased to exist, the High Priest was anointed and virtually took the place of the king.[2] Kings and High Priests, then, were spoken of as 'the Lord's Anointed' or 'the Anointed Ones'.

In several 'messianic' passages which refer to the coming of the future kingdom no mention is made at all of a leader or else it is quite incidental; the really important thing is the kingly rule of God. Elsewhere it is made plain that this kingly rule of God will be realized in the rule of a divinely chosen and divinely endowed king. There was a strong tradition, originating no doubt in God's promise to David recorded in II Samuel 7 and fostered by the prophets of the south, that this ruler of the coming kingdom would be of the House of David (cf. Micah 5.2ff; Isa. 11.1ff; Jer. 23.5ff, etc.); he is not given the name 'Messiah', but 'David' or 'scion of David', the allusion being to an actual historical kingship, a restoration of the Davidic line. The majority of the 'messianic' passages, however, are post-exilic, but even here the thought is still that of a 'scion of David's House' anointed and set apart for the fulfilment of God's own special purpose. It is in this sense that we are to understand, for example, the allusion to Zerubbabel as 'the Branch' (Zech. 3.8; 6.12); and no doubt his symbolic name ('a shoot out of Babylon') facilitated his association with the 'messianic' hopes of a restoration of David's line.

The characteristic view of the future hope during the post-exilic period continued to be that of a kingdom which would be

---

[1] E.g. Saul in I Sam. 10.1, David in I Sam. 16.13, etc.
[2] This is reflected in such post-exilic passages as Ex. 29.7; Lev. 8.12.

this-worldly, national and political by whose means Israel would be delivered from her enemies—the Babylonians, the Persians, the Seleucids, the Romans. It is true that in Deutero-Isaiah, for example, this future hope becomes increasingly other-worldly and transcendent, and deliverance is seen to come from the miraculous workings of God, but the political and national hope continued to hold its place in the popular view of the masses right on through the inter-testamental period.

A tension, however, had already been set up between this-worldly, national and political elements on the one hand, and other-worldly, universal and transcendent elements on the other which could not easily be resolved. This tension was greatly increased by the influence on Hebrew thought of Persian ideas and in particular the dualistic view of the world in which 'this age' was set over against 'the age to come'. Under this influence there grew up in Judaism, particularly in apocalyptic circles, an eschatology with new emphases, at once 'dualistic, cosmic, universalistic, transcendental and individualistic'.[1]

It is in connection with these two 'eschatologies' that the name 'Messiah' at last appears as a technical term, signifying the eschatological figure chosen by God to play a leading part in the coming of the kingdom. In each case a leader appears whose nature and function correspond to that future hope with which he is associated. The position is summed up by Dr S. Mowinckel in these words, 'The Messianic concepts of certain circles produced the picture of a Messiah who is predominantly this-worldly, national and political, whereas the views of other circles produced the picture of a predominantly transcendental, eternal and universal Messiah. . . . These two complexes of ideas are in part represented by different names, "Messiah" and "Son of Man".'[2]

[1] S. Mowinckel, *He That Cometh* (translated by G. W. Anderson), 1956, p. 271.
[2] *Ibid.*, p. 467.

In some writings these two conceptions are clearly distinguished; in others they are blended together; yet nowhere are they completely fused. Together they form part of that complex eschatology which is the background of the inter-testamental literature and also of the New Testament faith.

2. THE TRADITIONAL OR NATIONAL MESSIAH

A. *The Messiah not indispensable*

The traditional Old Testament hope of the coming of a 'messianic' prince as the leader of the Messianic Kingdom persists in this literature, but once again it is to be observed that the Messiah is not necessarily thought of as an indispensable figure. Indeed in a fairly considerable number of writings of this period (apocalyptic and otherwise), in which the messianic hope is ever in the forefront, the Messiah is not even mentioned. In the Book of Daniel, for example, the figure of the Messiah does not appear, although the term 'anointed one' occurs twice in two successive verses. In Dan. 9.25, 26 we read of 'an anointed one, a prince' and of another 'anointed one (who) shall be cut off', the references being presumably to the High Priests Jeshua and Onias III respectively. Similarly the figure of the Messiah is absent from I and II Maccabees, Tobit, the Wisdom of Solomon, Judith, Ben Sira, Jubilees, I Enoch 1-36, 91-104, the Assumption of Moses, I Baruch and II Enoch. The fact is that during the Persian period the hope of a Davidic Messiah had receded into the background and emphasis had come to be laid increasingly on the kingly rule of God in the future kingdom and on the prime necessity of keeping his holy Law. Moreover, the succession of High Priests who assumed the rôle of prince was not such as to inspire men with hopes of leadership from that source in the coming kingdom.

B. *The Levitic Messiah*

But such hopes were deeply stirred in many hearts during the period of the Maccabees and Hasmoneans, descendants of the House of Levi, when it seemed that at long last the messianic age was about to be realized. In particular the hopes of the people came to be centred in Simon, successor of Judas Maccabaeus. In the year 141 B.C. Simon was acknowledged by the people as 'ruler and high priest for ever', the first Maccabee to be so recognized.[1] Some scholars have found in Psalm 110.1-4 an acrostic on his name, indicating the regard in which he was held, but this is unlikely. The blessedness of his reign is described in characteristically messianic terms in I Maccabees 14.8ff. But neither here nor elsewhere is he referred to as the Messiah. The glories of the House of Levi were continued in the reign of his son, John Hyrcanus, to whom some scholars see a reference in the Testament of Levi 8.14, 'A king shall arise in Judah and shall establish a new priesthood'. Other scholars, however, see in these words a reference not to the House of Levi but to the House of Zadok which, as we shall see, held an honoured place among the Covenanters of Qumran. Whether this be so or not, there is no reference here to Hyrcanus as the Messiah.

But the Testaments of the Twelve Patriarchs, written during this period, indicate that in some circles at least hope was expressed in the coming of a Messiah from the House of Levi. This is made explicit in two passages, the Testament of Reuben 6.5-12 and the Testament of Levi 18.2ff. The second of these passages reads thus:

'Then shall the Lord raise up a new priest.
And to him all the words of the Lord shall be revealed;

[1] See p. 31.

And he shall execute a righteous judgment upon the earth for a
    multitude of days.
And his star shall arise in heaven as of a king.
Lighting up the light of knowledge as the sun the day,
And he shall be magnified in the world.
And he shall shine forth as the sun on the earth,
And shall remove all darkness from under heaven,
And there shall be peace in all the earth' (18.2-4).

It seems very unlikely that the writer had in mind any identification with an historical person such as Hyrcanus; it is not
certain indeed whether he had in mind even a future Hasmonean
Messiah for, in the words of H. H. Rowley, 'the functions assigned
to the Messiah from Levi go beyond the achievements of the
Hasmoneans, but it is possible that the author idealized a conception which was based on what had been done by the Hasmoneans and thought of a coming priest who would overthrow
all the forces of evil'.[1] Whatever the identity of the Messiah may
be, it seems certain that the glories of the Maccabean and Hasmonean House had inspired at least some among the people with
the hope of a Messiah from the tribe of Levi in whom they saw
many of those traits long associated with the Messiah from the
tribe of Judah. But disillusionment at last set in as the people
witnessed the increasing secularization of the High Priesthood,
and the old hope of a Davidic Messiah began to reassert
itself.

c. *The Davidic Messiah*

The hope in a Davidic Messiah is seen most clearly in two
writings of this period, the Testaments of the Twelve Patriarchs
and the Psalms of Solomon. The Testaments raise serious problems of a critical nature into which it is impossible here to

[1] *Jewish Apocalyptic and the Dead Sea Scrolls*, 1957, pp. 12-13.

enter. But in at least three passages, it has been argued,[1] belief in a Davidic Messiah can be attested. These are the Testament of Judah 17.5-6; 22.2-3; 24.1ff. In the last of these passages we read with reference to Judah:

'Then shall the sceptre of my kingdom shine forth;
And from your root shall arise a stem;
And from it shall grow a rod of righteousness to the Gentiles;
To judge and to save all that call upon the Lord.'

The evidence of the Testaments, then, seems to indicate that the author of this book believed in the emergence not of one Messiah but of two, a Davidic Messiah who would rule as king in the coming kingdom and a Levitic Messiah who would act as priest.[2] So exalted is the author's view of the priesthood that the Messiah of Levi here takes precedence over the Messiah of David. We observe that in the Book of Jubilees, though no Messiah of Levi is mentioned but only a vague hope in the coming of a Davidic prince, the greatness ascribed to Levi corresponds closely to that of the Testaments (cf. Jubilees 31.13-20).

But the chief source of this teaching concerning a Davidic Messiah is the Psalms of Solomon, which belong to the middle of the first century B.C. Psalm 18 speaks of a Messiah, though no actual identification is made with David's line. Psalm 17, however, makes this reference quite specific. The figure of the Davidic Messiah is introduced in these words, 'Behold, O Lord, and raise up unto them their king, the Son of David' (17.23). Having shattered unrighteous rulers and purged Jerusalem from her enemies, he will gather together all the tribes and distribute them throughout the land as in former times. The heathen nations will be made to serve under his yoke, and he will rule over his own

[1] Cf. G. R. Beasley-Murray, *Journal of Theological Studies,* xlviii, 1947, pp. 1ff.
[2] For reference to two Messiahs in the Dead Sea Scrolls, see pp. 127ff.

people in righteousness and wisdom; in their national assemblies his word will be as the word of an angel. He will allow no unrighteousness to lodge in their midst; his subjects will be all holy and sons of God.

'And he himself (will be) pure from sin, so that he may rule a
    great people.
He will rebuke rulers, and remove sinners by the might of his
    word;
And (relying) upon his God, throughout his days he will not
    stumble;
For God will make him mighty by means of (his) holy spirit'
    (17.41-42).

Several things become clear from this picture of the Davidic Messiah ruling in his kingdom. The first is that he is a thoroughly human figure who is above all a ruler and a king who champions the cause of his people Israel. In Psalm 17.36 the name 'Messiah' is used for the first time in this literature as the title of the coming king; this indicates that at last the expression 'Messiah' in its technical sense is brought into relation to the messianic concept. Moreover, the religious and moral side of his character is strongly stressed. Not only is he righteous and pure from sin, his reliance is placed upon his God and his hope is in the Lord. The kingdom which he establishes and which will know no end is viewed along familiar lines, for it is an earthly kingdom with Jerusalem as its centre.

Throughout the rest of this century and right on into the first century of the Christian era the figure of the Messianic king lived on in the hearts of many people, as the New Testament itself makes only too clear. But no longer was he thought of as coming after God had established his kingdom; rather was he God's instrument in the establishment of it, and his foremost task was the destruction of God's enemies from the face of the earth.

During this period there arose, particularly in certain apocalyptic circles, a belief in an interim Messianic Kingdom at the close of which the Messiah would die and God himself would reign supreme (cf. II Esdras 7.29f; 12.31f; II Baruch 30.1ff). But in the popular imagination increasing stress was laid on the national and political aspects of his work, and the future hope was viewed, particularly in times of persecution and national unrest, in terms of deliverance from the alien power of Rome (cf. Matt. 21.9). The Messiah was regarded by many as a military deliverer of the Zealot type who would rid the country of their hated enemy. And so there arose a series of 'false Messiahs' who incited the people against the common foe—Hezekiah the 'brigand' whom Herod executed, his son Judas the Galilean and his brother Menahem, the prophet Theudas in the time of the procurator Cuspius Fadus (cf. Acts 5.36), the Egyptian Jew who was put to death by the procurator Felix (cf. Acts 21.38), another Jew who led his followers out into the wilderness in the time of Festus, and Simon bar Kochba whose revolt was quelled in A.D. 135.

D. *The Messiah and the Dead Sea Scrolls*

We have already seen evidence for believing that the writer of the Testaments of the Twelve Patriarchs looked forward to the coming of two Messiahs, one priestly and the other kingly. This belief, it would seem, was shared by the Covenanters of Qumran where, incidentally, fragments of an earlier form of the Testament of Levi, written in Aramaic, have been found. In the Zadokite Fragments,[1] which undoubtedly belong to the same milieu though discovered at a much earlier date, reference is made to the coming of a Messiah [*sic*] of Aaron and Israel, apparently forty years after the 'gathering in' of the Teacher of Righteousness. The evidence of the Dead Sea Scrolls strongly suggests that the singular word here was originally read as a

[1] This work is also known as the Damascus Document.

plural and that the expectation of the writer was for a Messiah of Aaron (i.e. a priestly Messiah) and a Messiah of Israel (i.e. a kingly Messiah, presumably Davidic). This at least is the belief expressed in the scrolls themselves. There it is stated that the members of the community shall continue to live according to the original discipline 'until there shall come a prophet and the Messiahs of Aaron and Israel' (Manual of Discipline, col. ix, line 11). Some scholars would here give the translation 'anointed one' for 'Messiahs' and make the phrase refer simply to the restoration of the true line of Aaronic priests and Davidic kings. But the indications are that two Messiahs are expected whose coming would mark the new era for which the Covenanters had hoped and prayed. The Teacher of Righteousness, it would seem, was to be a forerunner of the Messiah; on his death would follow forty years of bitter conflict between 'the sons of light and the sons of darkness' at the close of which the messianic age would dawn.

The belief of the Covenanters in a kingly and military Messiah was in keeping with the traditional hopes of the nation and had the support of many Old Testament prophecies. But, unlike the writer of the Testaments, their belief in a priestly Messiah could not have arisen out of admiration for the Hasmonean priestly House of Levi, for they themselves were loyal sons of Zadok and looked forward to the coming of a priestly Messiah of Zadok's line which alone represented the true High Priestly office.

Such a belief in a priestly leader and a kingly leader would find precedent in the joint leadership of Joshua and Zerubbabel, the two 'sons of oil', in the early days of the Second Temple (cf. Zechariah 3-4). Moreover, in the scrolls as in the Testaments, the priestly Messiah is given precedence over the kingly Messiah and recalls the relative positions of priest and king in the ideal commonwealth of Ezekiel 40-48. This is indicated in a collection of benedictions from Cave I in which blessings are given, one for the High Priest and one for the 'prince of the congregation'. The subordination of the kingly Messiah is made plain in fragments from the same Cave relating to a 'Messianic Banquet'. There we read, 'Let no one begin to eat bread or drink wine before the priest, for it is his province to bless the first mouthful of bread and wine and to stretch forth his hands first upon the bread. Thereafter the Messiah of Israel may stretch forth his hands upon the bread.'

Some scholars have seen in the scrolls evidence for the resurrection of the Teacher of Righteousness after the forty years' travail and on the eve of the messianic age. If this is so, it is possible that the Covenanters thought of him in the same way in which popular tradition thought of Elijah, as a forerunner of the Messiah, although there is no indication at all that he is in any way to be identified with that prophet.

E. *Jesus and the Messiah*

At the beginning of the Christian era the vast majority of the Jews shared the belief in the coming of a mighty warrior-Messiah of David's line. The Qumran Covenanters looked forward eagerly to the time when such a Messiah would lead them forth in the great final battle between 'the sons of darkness' and 'the sons of light'. The Zealots,*too, were ready at any moment to flock to his standard and to fight by his side with naked sword.

Small wonder that Jesus, from the time of his temptation onwards, not only refused to proclaim himself Messiah but discouraged others from using the title of him. He knew himself to be such, and later his disciples knew also (cf. Mark 8.29), but not until near the end of his life, when he stood before the High Priest, did he acknowledge openly his messiahship (Mark 14.61f).[1]

[1] According to the Fourth Gospel, however, his messiahship is acknowledged from the beginning of his public ministry (John 1.41, 49).

To have done so earlier would have led to complete misunderstanding not only on the part of the people, but even on the part of his own disciples. How different was his interpretation from that of the people of his day. Not for him the rôle of the mighty warrior, gaining his kingdom by bloodshed and war. His kingdom would come not by taking life but by giving it. At Caesarea Philippi, in reply to Peter's words 'Thou art the Messiah', he made it clear that his messiahship would be fulfilled only in terms of the Suffering Servant who would 'give his life a ransom for many' (Mark 10.45).[1] Such a correlation of these ideas was something new in Judaism. True, 'Suffering Servant' and 'Kingly Messiah' may have had common roots in the royal cultic rites as reflected, for example, in the Psalter, as scholars have suggested; but as H. H. Rowley remarks, 'There is no serious evidence of the bringing together of the concepts of the Suffering Servant and the Davidic Messiah before the Christian era . . . the two concepts were brought together in the thought and teaching of Jesus.'[2] Here was a divine imperative from which he could not shrink. 'Jesus did not believe Himself to be the Messiah, *although* He had to suffer. He believed Himself to be the Messiah, *because* He had to suffer.'[3] This message of a crucified Messiah was to the Jews a stumbling-block and to the Gentiles foolishness, but to 'those who are called' it was the power and the wisdom of God (cf. I Cor. 1.23f).

3. THE TRANSCENDENT MESSIAH AND THE SON OF MAN

Prior to the year 200 B.C., as we have already seen, there had been growing up among the Jews an eschatology in many ways

[1] For a fuller statement concerning the relation of the Suffering Servant to the Son of Man and the Messiah, see pp. 138ff.

[2] Essay on 'The Suffering Servant and the Davidic Messiah' in *The Servant of the Lord*, 1952, p. 85.

[3] Goguel, *Life of Jesus*, E.T. 1933, p. 392, quoted by A. M. Hunter, *Introducing New Testament Theology*, 1957, p. 44.

different from the national and political conception of the Old Testament, characterized chiefly by a dualistic view of the universe, a belief in the resurrection and a transcendental view of the 'Golden Age'. These new ideas continued to permeate Jewish thought and were familiar and popular some time before the beginning of the Christian era. Their influence on men's understanding of the Messiah began to be felt at an early stage, even in writings where the old national and political ideas were dominant. Transcendent characteristics tended to attach themselves to his person; not only was he the military hero who would restore the Jewish State and establish the kingdom on earth, he was the king of peace under whose rule Paradise would return to the earth (Test. of Levi 18.10f; cf. Sibylline Oracles Bk. V, II Esdras, II Baruch). In certain apocalyptic circles, however, the influence of these ideas went further, for there the Messiah appears as a genuinely transcendent king. Of particular importance is the emergence of a mysterious figure called 'the Man' or 'the Son of Man' who, though different in origin and in characteristics from the traditional Jewish Messiah, came to have a deep influence on popular messianic hopes.

A. *The apocalyptic Son of Man*

The figure of the Son of Man appears, for the first time in the apocalyptic literature, in Dan. 7.13ff which tells of 'one like unto a son of man' coming with the clouds of heaven to be presented before 'the ancient of days'. It is clear from a reading of this passage that the figure here mentioned is not the Messiah and indeed that he is not an individual at all, but rather a symbol for the glorified Israel in the coming eschatological kingdom. In 7.18 the Son of Man is identified with 'the saints of the Most High', and this is supported by the symbolism of the passage; there the dominion of four kingdoms, symbolized by four beasts which emerge from the depth of the sea, passes over to the kingdom of the saints or ideal people of God, symbolized by a heavenly being in human form, thus differentiating it from the other kingdoms. Theirs is an everlasting dominion and a kingdom which will not be destroyed.

Scholars have pointed out that the vision in Daniel 7 has features which recall the Book of Ezekiel (cf. ch. 1) where the phrase 'son of man' occurs over 100 times signifying 'man' both in his creaturely weakness and in his glorious place in God's creation (cf. also Ps. 8.4, 5). Others have found connections between the Son of Man of Daniel and the Suffering Servant of Deutero-Isaiah where, in each case, the people of God are 'the wise' who will make 'the many' righteous.[1] Others again have traced the Son of Man idea to mythological sources in current oriental thought and in this way attempt to explain certain features which could not otherwise be understood.[2]

The next stage in the development of this idea is to be found in the Similitudes of Enoch (I Enoch 37-71) which is probably to be dated in the Maccabean age. There has been much controversy over the question of suggested Christian interpolations, but there seems good reason for believing that the book is a literary unity and that the so-called interpolations are in fact part of the text. The Son of Man is here presented as a heavenly being with no prior earthly existence at all; but he is pre-existent (48.3), having been created by God before the foundation of the world and hidden by him from the beginning (48.6; 62.7); he is a divine creature whose face is 'full of graciousness, like one of the holy angels' (46.1), upon whom God bestows his own divine glory (61.8). But although he is divine, he may yet be thought of as the typical or ideal man who, as 'the Elect One', stands at the head of 'the elect ones' in the heavenly kingdom. His character is marked by wisdom, understanding and righteousness, and the righteous will one day be exalted to be with him. With him are hidden all

[1] See further pp. 138f. [2] See pp. 134f.

the secrets of the universe (52.1ff). But the greatest secret is the Son of Man himself who remains hidden, but will one day be revealed. Indeed this secret has been revealed already to the elect (48.7). The time will come when 'the Righteous One shall appear before the eyes of the righteous' (38.2) in all his splendour and be seated on the throne of God's glory (61.8). He will stand before God as judge of heaven and earth, of angels as well as of men, of the dead as well as of the living (61.8). His appearing will bring deliverance to the godly (48.4ff) and they will share in the kingdom of the Son of Man (61.5).

It has been claimed that this figure of the Son of Man is an imaginative development of that already given in Daniel 7. This view is supported by the fact that the description of God's throne in I Enoch 71.7ff (cf. also 14.18f) is largely derived from Ezekiel 1 and Daniel 7 and that the Son of Man passages read like a Midrash or commentary on Daniel 7. Dr T. W. Manson interprets the Son of Man here as a collective symbol, as in Daniel 7, and believes that the same interpretation applies to the other names by which he is called, 'the Righteous One', 'the Elect One' and 'the Anointed One'.[1] In a later article[2] the same author sees in this concept both a collective and an individual reference. The collective idea finds expression in the Remnant; the individual idea in two personalities—Enoch himself (cf. I Enoch 71.14) who is regarded as the nucleus of the group of the elect ones, and the Messiah who will in the end vindicate the saints. Dr H. H. Rowley denies any reference here to the Messiah and recognizes in this figure 'the personifying of the Danielic concept of the Son of Man in a supramundane person who should be the representative and head of the kingdom that concept symbolized, and who should come down to dwell with men'.[3] Others, like Dr S. Mowinckel,

[1] Cf. *The Teaching of Jesus*, 2nd edition, 1935, pp. 228f.
[2] Cf. *Bulletin of the John Rylands Library*, xxxii. 1949-50, pp. 178ff.
[3] *The Relevance of Apocalyptic*, 1944, p. 57. See also 'The Suffering Servant and the Davidic Messiah' in *The Servant of the Lord*, 1952, p. 76.

maintain that behind the Son of Man, as in Daniel 7, stands the figure of the Heavenly Man or the Primordial Man to be found in oriental mythology and that in I Enoch the effects of this influence are much more obvious than in the case of Daniel 7.

The figure of the Son of Man appears again in the post-Christian apocalyptic writings, II Esdras and the Sibylline Oracles, Bk. V, both of which are influenced by the vision and the language of Daniel 7.13ff. Here the figure of the Son of Man is in many respects in line with that given in the Similitudes of Enoch. He is presented, however, as the Messiah; but this is no human figure of David's line; he is a pre-existent, transcendent figure who will one day appear before the righteous in all his glory. As in the Similitudes of Enoch so here, everything that pertains to 'the Man', as he is called, is a divine secret, for 'just as one can neither seek out nor know what is in the deep of the sea, even so can no one upon earth see my Son, but in the time of his day' (II Esdras 13.52). In that day he will come flying with the clouds of heaven (13.3f) or will emerge from the depths of the sea (13.51f). In him the mysteries of God's purpose are concealed, but when he sits on the throne of God's glory what is hidden will at last be revealed.

The popularity of this transcendent figure was no doubt much more restricted than the new eschatology of which it formed a part, but its influence would be felt outside the confined apocalyptic circle to which it belonged. To what extent, however, this influence was felt, it is impossible to say. In course of time in the Christian era, it was regarded with increasing disfavour in orthodox Jewish circles, no doubt partly because of its use among the Christians, and found practically no place in subsequent Jewish theology.

B. *The oriental background*

Christian theological presuppositions apart, there is very little in this body of literature to remind the reader of the traditional Jewish eschatology with its belief in a national, historical and political Messiah. Indeed the apocalyptic Son of Man is as foreign to the old eschatology as it is native to the new transcendental eschatology here presented. It has been argued that, since this new teaching concerning the last things may well have come into Judaism by way of Persian influence, those ideas relating to the Son of Man may also have come originally from that same source.

Throughout the oriental and Hellenistic world the belief was widespread in a Primordial Man whose qualities and properties were, in some respects at any rate, strikingly similar to those of the Son of Man of Jewish apocalyptic. This belief assumed many different forms throughout the eastern world, but there is good reason to believe that they can be traced back to corresponding ideas in the Persian or Iranian system, where the figure of the Primordial Man plays an important part in the unfolding of 'the last things'. Dr S. Mowinckel indeed claims that 'recent research has made it increasingly clear that the Jewish conception of "the Man" or "the Son of Man" is a Jewish variant of the oriental, cosmological, eschatological myth of Anthropos'.[1] Those features in the apocalyptic Son of Man which cannot find explanation in terms of Old Testament ideas, he says, find a full explanation in what is known about the Primordial Man such as his rising from the sea, his rôle as king of Paradise, and his connection with creation.

But although there are striking similarities between the two conceptions, there are important differences which show that, if the apocalyptists took over the idea, they at the same time made significant changes in line with their own religious heritage. In Daniel 7, for example, much of the mythological content has been removed, and the mythology that remains is only incidental to

[1] *Op. cit.*, p. 425.

the symbolism which portrays the purpose of God through his saints. In the Similitudes of Enoch the presence of mythological elements is more obvious, but even here mythology has been to some considerable extent assimilated to the ideas of the Old Testament. Whatever influence this idea of the Primordial Man may have had on Jewish thought it certainly was not taken over at any one period or from any one source, but came from many quarters and in different forms and was swept up, as it were, into the current of apocalyptic hope. It is unlikely indeed that there was any conscious borrowing of the idea or any awareness of its origin in oriental mythology, especially when in due course it came to be associated with the Jewish idea of the Messiah.

c. *The Son of Man as Messiah*

It is most probable that the ideas of the Son of Man and the Messiah had different origins and represent two quite separate conceptions of the inauguration of the coming kingdom, and that, for the vast majority of Jewish people, they had little or no connection with each other. They indicate two distinct strands of expectation which, in the course of the years, became intertwined in the thought of a relatively small group of apocalyptic writers, so that 'there emerged a Messianic figure both eternal and transcendental, and also historical and human, in an eschatology both historical and also supra-historical and absolute'.[1]

This development is evident from a comparison of Daniel 7 (*c.* 165 B.C.) and II Esdras 13 (*c.* A.D. 90). In the former passage, as has been indicated already, no mention is made at all of the Messiah as the deliverer of his people, and certainly the Son of Man who appears there does not assume this rôle. In II Esdras the great deliverer of the coming age is known as the Son of Man and has many characteristics known to belong to that transcendent figure (cf. 13.3ff), but at the same time he is called 'my

[1] S. Mowinckel, *op. cit.*, p. 436.

Messiah' or 'my son the Messiah' (7.28-29) who 'shall spring from the seed of David' (12.32). He is given the messianic title 'my servant'[1] (7.28; 13.32, etc.) and reveals a number of characteristics which belong to the national hope associated with that name.[2]

The tension which developed between this-worldly and other-worldly elements, represented by the names 'Messiah' and 'Son of Man', was relieved in some writings by the introduction of an interim kingdom, a 'Millennium', in which, after a preliminary judgment, the Messiah would reign upon the earth for 1,000 years (cf. II Enoch 32.2-33.2; Rev. 20.4-7). Sometimes the duration is 400 years (cf. II Esdras 7.28); at other times the kingdom lasts for an indefinite period (cf. II Baruch 40.3). This interim kingdom marks the close of the present aeon and is itself followed by the general judgment, the destruction of the world, the new creation, the resurrection[3] and the beginning of the new age of bliss.[4] The introduction of this idea of a Millennium is in itself an indication of that compromise which the apocalyptic writers adopted between these two strands of expectation and shows how the idea of the Messiah, albeit in supra-mundane form, not only survived but triumphed over the powerful influence of the concept of the Son of Man.

There is no small disagreement among scholars concerning the relationship between the Son of Man and the Messiah in the Similitudes of Enoch. Dr H. H. Rowley, for example, asserts that 'there is no evidence that the Son of Man was identified with the Messiah until the time of Jesus'.[5] He supports this by pointing out that, although Jesus did not apply the term 'Messiah' to himself

---

[1] The Latin phrase *filius meus* no doubt reflects the Greek word *pais* which may mean either 'son' or 'servant'. The latter meaning is more common in later use and probably represents the correct rendering of the original text; cf. Acts 3.13 (RV margin).

[2] Cf. 13.33ff; also II Baruch 29.3; 30.1; 39.7; 40.1; 70.9; 72.2.

[3] Rev. 20.4 mentions also a first resurrection at the beginning of the millennial reign of Christ.

[4] See further pp. 150f.   [5] *Op. cit.*, p. 29.

during his ministry and indeed charged his disciples to tell no man that he was, he nevertheless openly used the expression 'Son of Man' of himself. In the Similitudes of Enoch, he maintains, the Son of Man is not equated with the Messiah, for here we have no human deliverer who can in any way be associated with the Old Testament hope, but a purely transcendent figure. Others, like W. F. Albright, argue that even before the time of Jesus there was a certain amount of fusion between the two figures. It is of interest to note that the writer of I Enoch attaches to the transcendent Son of Man certain characteristics which were already familiar to the tradition of the Messiah; he is righteous and wise, he is chosen of God, he receives the homage of kings, he is a light to the Gentiles and is actually called 'the Anointed One' of God (48.10; 52.4). These references do not necessarily connect him with the Davidic earthly Messiah, and indeed the whole picture rules this out, but they may indicate that even thus early the title 'Son of Man' has acquired a 'messianic' ring. Even if this is so, however, this relation between the Son of Man and the Messiah would be largely confined to that small circle of apocalyptists represented by the writer of this book.

D. *Suffering and death*

Some scholars maintain that Daniel's visions were dependent originally on the Servant passages in Deutero-Isaiah and that the Son of Man in the one is representative of the Suffering Servant in the other. In each case reference is made to 'the wise' (Isa. 52.13; Dan. 12.3) who make 'the many' righteous (Isa. 53.11; Dan. 12.3) and who suffer in obedience to the will of God (Isa. 53.3ff; Dan. 11.33). Dr F. F. Bruce argues[1] that the Covenanters of Qumran, for example, interpreted their mission in terms of the 'unitive exegesis' of Deutero-Isaiah and Daniel. They described themselves as 'the wise'

[1] *New Testament Studies*, vol. 2, no. 3, pp. 176ff.

(Hebrew *maskilim*) and 'the saints of the Most High' (cf. Dan. 7.18) who, by submission and endurance, would effect atonement for the sin of the people in the manner of the Suffering Servant of the Lord. But in their interpretation of them, 'Son of Man' and 'Servant of the Lord' remained societary figures, for the work of expiation which they set themselves to do was the work not of any one member, not even the Messiah in their midst, but of the whole community. There is evidence, moreover, that a messianic interpretation of the Servant may be intended in the strange variant reading of Isa. 52.14 in the St Mark's (A) Scroll: 'I have anointed (Heb. *mashachti*) his face more than any man.' If this is so the context indicates that the reference is probably to the *priestly* and not to the *kingly* Messiah.

It is true that in I Enoch expressions from the Servant Poems of Deutero-Isaiah are used to describe the glory of the Son of Man, as in 48.4 where it is said that 'he shall be a light of the Gentiles' (Isa. 42.6; 49.6; cf. Luke 2.32). But this influence does not extend beyond the use of phrases; the content of the Servant Songs is nowhere read into the character and work of the Son of Man. The picture of the Servant which lies behind the Son of Man in the apocalyptic literature is a totally different concept from that which we find in Deutero-Isaiah where the Servant, by means of his vicarious suffering and death, justifies the many and bears their iniquities (Isa. 53.11).

Mention might be made here of the interpretation of the Servant in the Targum of Isaiah 52.13-53.12. There the Servant is identified with the Messiah, but the whole passage is re-interpreted in such a way that it is impossible to recognize the figure of the Old Testament text. His sufferings, pain and death are transferred to the enemies of Israel, and the Servant-Messiah appears as the mighty conqueror who triumphs over all his foes!

In II Esdras 7.29 we read of the death of the Messiah at

the end of the interim kingdom; this is natural, for the Messiah, like all other created beings, must die. But no reference is made here or elsewhere in the book to a vicarious, atoning death. The deliverance which the Son of Man brings is not salvation from the power of sin, but deliverance from the oppression of their enemies. He is the terrible judge of sinners, not the Saviour of men's souls.

E. *Jesus and the Son of Man*

The Synoptic Gospels indicate that Jesus not only used the expression 'Son of Man' of himself, but actually preferred its use to that of any other messianic title. It was in terms of the Son of Man that he sought to understand and to interpret his messiah-ship throughout his public ministry. But his interpretation was vastly different from any that had gone before.

There can be little doubt that, in his choice of this title, Jesus was deeply influenced by Dan. 7.13ff which reads, 'There came with the clouds of heaven one like unto a son of man. . . . And there was given him dominion, and glory, and a kingdom, that all the peoples, nations, and languages should serve him.' Taking up this expression he applied it as a title to himself, in whose person and ministry the kingdom was to be expressed. In so doing he asserted that to belong to him was to belong to the kingdom, for where he was the kingdom was present among men. He did not simply herald its coming, he embodied it in his own person, and in his public ministry of preaching and healing and casting out demons he demonstrated that it was present and operative in men's midst. 'If I by the finger of God cast out devils, then is the kingdom of God come upon you' (Luke 11.20).

But the kingdom, like the One in whom it was embodied, remained hidden and a mystery (Mark 4.11) until its secret would be revealed. This mystery was indeed part of the 'Messianic Secret' involved in Jesus' conception of himself as the Son of

Man. His kingdom was not of this world and so, as we have seen, he avoided the use of the term 'Messiah' and discouraged others from using it of him. But the time was coming when the mystery of the kingdom would be revealed. With the resurrection of the Son of Man and the coming of the Spirit it would at last become an open secret and the kingdom would come 'with power' (Mark 9.1; cf. Rom. 1.4). The Son of Man would be exalted and be seen 'coming with the clouds of heaven' (Mark 14.62); the kingdom would be consummated in his coming again to reign.

Thus it was that to Jesus death was necessary to the fulfilment of God's purpose in him, for 'between the coming of the Kingdom as a "mystery" and its coming "with power" lies the Cross. . . . The Cross was inevitable if the "mystery" was to become an open secret. Jesus died in order that the Kingdom might come "with power".'[1] Here we come to the very heart of Jesus' understanding of his messiahship—'The Son of man must suffer . . . and be killed, and after three days rise again' (Mark 8.31). The Cross was not a mistake or an accident; it was part of the predetermined counsel of God. The sovereign Son of Man was the Suffering Servant of the Lord.

It is speculative in the extreme to try to assess how far Jesus' thinking in this connection was influenced by the teaching of the apocalyptic writings referred to above; but it is quite clear that his association of the Suffering Servant with the Son of Man did not originate in these esoteric circles. If we are to seek any source at all other than his own consciousness of mission, then it is perhaps again to the Book of Daniel that we must turn. In Mark 1.14f we read, 'Jesus came into Galilee, preaching the gospel of God, and saying, The time is fulfilled, and the kingdom of God is at hand (cf. Dan. 2.44): repent ye, and believe in the gospel (cf. Isa. 61.1ff)'. By so speaking Jesus showed a penetrating insight into the relationship between Daniel and Deutero-Isaiah

[1] A. M. Hunter, *Introducing New Testament Theology*, 1957, p. 45.

and, by implication, between the Son of Man and the Suffering Servant. Like the Covenanters of Qumran he interpreted his mission in terms of a 'unitive exegesis' of these two books, but unlike them he saw the fulfilment of these prophetic words in himself—in his life and death and resurrection, in the coming of the Spirit, in the life of the Church and in his coming again to reign.[1] The Messiah-Son of Man was the Suffering Servant of the Lord through whose sacrifice the kingdom would come and the will of God be done on earth as it was in heaven.

[1] Compare, however, the argument of T. W. Manson who maintains that, even on the lips of Jesus, the expression 'Son of Man' is to be understood in a societary sense and signifies an ideal figure standing for 'the manifestation of the Kingdom of God on earth in a people wholly devoted to their heavenly King' (*The Teaching of Jesus*, p. 227). But during the course of his ministry this figure came to be individualized so that the title became a designation of himself.

7

The Resurrection and the Life Beyond

IN very many ways the apocalyptic literature serves as a bridge between the Old Testament and the New Testament, and this is perhaps nowhere more clearly shown than in its belief concerning the life beyond death. Much of the teaching of the New Testament in this respect is inexplicable simply in terms of the Old Testament background, but it can be seen in its true light within the setting of apocalyptic thought. Of particular significance is its teaching concerning the resurrection from the dead.

According to ancient Hebrew 'psychology' man's nature is the product of two factors, 'the breath-soul (Hebrew *nephesh*) which is the principle of life, and the complex of physical organs which this animates. Separate them, and man ceases to be, in any real sense of personality.'[1] That is, man is not constituted of three 'parts' called body, mind and spirit or body, soul and spirit; nor is he constituted simply of two 'parts', body and soul. He is a unity of personality whose dissolution means the end of life in any true sense of that word. For a time a man, it is true, may conceivably live on in the elements of his body which possess psychical and not merely physical properties. But with the departure of his *nephesh* a man's life ebbs away and he ceases to be a living 'person'. What survives death is not a man's soul or

[1] H. Wheeler Robinson, *Religious Ideas of the Old Testament*, 1913, p. 83.

spirit, but his shade or ghost, a kind of 'double' of the once living man, retaining a shadowy resemblance to its once living counterpart, but bereft of that personal existence which once characterized the man.

For long centuries the belief prevailed that at death a man's shade or ghost went to Sheol, situated beneath the earth or beneath the great cosmic ocean on which the earth stood, a land of forgetfulness, darkness and despair, having no continuity with life upon the earth (cf. Job 10.21f). At a later stage of Hebrew thought the belief was expressed that God's power and influence could be felt even in Sheol (Ps. 139.8), but for the most part the accepted view was that Sheol lay beyond his jurisdiction (Pss. 30.9f; 115.17, etc.). In some passages the shade of the departed, especially if he were a man of outstanding renown like Samuel, was credited with superhuman powers and was believed to possess knowledge of the past and of the future as well (I Sam. 28.8ff), but for the ordinary run of men it was a land of no-return (cf. II Sam. 12.23; Job 7.9) where 'the dead know nothing, neither have they any more a reward . . . there is no work or thought or knowledge or wisdom in Sheol, whither thou goest' (Eccles. 9.5, 10). All moral distinctions ceased to exist, for in Sheol 'one fate comes to all, to the righteous and the wicked' (Eccles. 9.2).

Scholars have differed widely in their interpretation of such passages as Job 14.13-15 and 19.25-27 in which the writer's faith reaches out in hope for vindication beyond the bounds of human flesh, and Psalms 16, 49, 73 and 78 in which the problem of the prosperity of the wicked and the suffering of the righteous turns the psalmists' thoughts to that continuing fellowship with God at whose right hand there are 'pleasures for evermore'. There is certainly no clearly defined doctrine of a life beyond death encountered here, but at best only a glimmering of hope. This hope, however, was such that it could reach its logical conclusion only in a belief in a future life, and it is to the credit of the apocalyptists that they were the first to arrive at this conclusion in the doctrine of the resurrection from the dead.

I. THE RESURRECTION, ITS ORIGIN AND DEVELOPMENT

A. *The Old Testament preparation*

According to the prophets of the Old Testament the hope for the future lay in the nation and in the coming kingdom which God would establish upon the earth; its glories would be shared by those righteous Israelites who were living at that time and also, some thought, by the Gentiles who would come to acknowledge Israel as the chosen people of God. This kingdom was an ever-lasting kingdom whose members would share the blessings of a ripe old age, like the patriarchs of old.

But the pious in Israel could not remain satisfied with such a belief. Already there was a growing conviction that the sense of fellowship which they enjoyed with God in this life could not surely come to an end with death, but that even in Sheol men might be able to praise him. With this there was growing up in Israel a new conception of religious individualism, associated particularly with Jeremiah, a man of deep personal religious experience. This emphasis was continued by Ezekiel who coupled with it a doctrine of individual retribution which declared that men are punished in proportion to their sin and rewarded in proportion to their righteousness during their lifetime here upon the earth. The problems raised by the contradiction between such a belief and the actual events of life are expressed in some of the Psalms and in the Book of Proverbs and find their classical expression in the Book of Job.

At long last a solution was reached which was to have a revolutionary effect on the religions both of Judaism and of Christianity.

Not only would the righteous nation share in the coming Messianic Kingdom; the righteous individual would share in it too, for the righteous dead would be raised in resurrection and would receive due recompense from the hand of God. This synthesis of the eschatologies of the nation and of the individual was brought about by the apocalyptists whose belief in a bodily resurrection made such a fusion possible.

B. *Its historical origin*

Perhaps the particular point at issue which helped finally to establish this belief would be the fact of the martyrdom of many righteous in Israel. Those who had suffered martyrdom must still in some way share in the ultimate triumph of God's people when he would at last establish his kingdom on the earth. There was felt to be a lacuna unless God brought back, raised up, those who had shown themselves worthy to take part in his kingly rule. For this reason those people must have bodies; the earth must give birth to them again.

Two Old Testament passages are of particular significance in this connection—Isaiah 24-27 and Daniel 12—both of which confirm that the historical origin of the resurrection in the Old Testament is one of selection, first of the very good (cf. Isa. 26.19) and then of the very good and the very bad (cf. Dan. 12.2-3). Isaiah 24-27, which reveals certain apocalyptic characteristics, is thought to be a late addition to the Book of Isaiah, dating possibly from the third or fourth century B.C. There we read, 'Thy dead shall arise: the inhabitants of the dust shall awake and shout for joy, for a dew of lights is thy dew, and the earth shall bring to life the shades' (Isa. 26.19). Some scholars take this, like Ezekiel's vision of the valley of dry bones, to refer to a national resurrection; but if in fact it refers to the actual resurrection of men's bodies, then this is the first occurrence of such a belief in the Old Testament. It is significant that in this passage only the pre-eminently righteous are raised to participate in the Messianic Kingdom which will be established on the earth. It has been suggested that this verse may refer to the time of Artaxerxes III (358-338 B.C.) when many Jews were martyred. If this be so, we may have here the very historical event which led to the formulation of the belief in a physical resurrection from the dead.

In Daniel 12 we are on surer historical ground, for this book was compiled in 165 B.C. in the time of Antiochus IV (Epiphanes). No doubt the resurrection belief here expressed arose out of the persecution preceding the Maccabean Revolt in which many Jews were martyred. There we read, 'And many of them that sleep in the dust of the earth shall awake, some to everlasting life and some to everlasting contempt' (Dan. 12.2). The day of God's deliverance was near at hand when his kingdom would be established on the earth. But many in Israel had laid down their lives in faithfulness to him; surely even death could not rob them of their portion. God would raise up these martyrs so that, together with the living, they might share in the blessings of his kingdom (cf. also II Macc. 7.9, 14, 23, 36). But others among Israel's enemies had died without receiving due recompense for their wickedness. They, too, would be raised to receive the punishment that was their due. Once more the principle of selection is seen at work, but now not only would the very good be raised for reward, the very bad would be raised for judgment. The shades of all other men would remain as before in the depths of dark Sheol.

c. *Subsequent developments*

Both these biblical conceptions of resurrection are to be found also in the extra-biblical apocalyptic books; but in the subsequent development occur many variations not all of which are clear to the reader, or even perhaps to the writers themselves!

The thought of Isaiah 24-27 is largely followed in I Enoch 6-36 (cf. also 37-71, 83-90, etc.) where only the righteous, presumably Israelites, are resurrected to take part in the Messianic Kingdom (25.4ff). The risen life is an organic development of the present life of righteousness (90.33). Here the wicked who have received punishment in this life will remain in Sheol everlastingly (22.13), but the wicked who have not received their due punishment on earth will be transferred as disembodied spirits from Sheol to Gehenna,[1] the place of torment.

A variation on the theme of Daniel 12.2 is to be found in the Noachic Fragments in I Enoch where it is at least implied that the righteous will be raised to share the blessings of the living righteous in the Messianic Kingdom (10.7, 20), and that the wicked, or some of them (67.8), will be resurrected for judgment and will suffer in the fires of Gehenna in body and spirit (67.8-9). In the Testament of Benjamin the patriarchs rise first to share in the earthly kingdom (10.6) and then the twelve sons of Jacob, each one over his own tribe (10.7). 'Then also *all* men shall rise, some unto glory and some unto shame' (10.8). This conception is still further developed in II Esdras which declares that there will be a general resurrection to be followed by a judgment which will be universal and final. The souls of the righteous and the wicked, being now united with the body, will be judged; 'and recompense shall follow, and the reward be made manifest' (7.35).

It has already been pointed out[2] that in certain apocryphal books, particularly the Wisdom of Solomon, the writers express a belief in the immortality of the soul and not the resurrection of the body. Among the apocalyptic writings the Book of Jubilees is of chief importance in this regard, as for example in 23.31, 'And their bones will rest in the earth, and their spirits will have much joy'. Jubilees in this regard, then, marks a breakaway from the firm conviction of the apocalyptic tradition.

[1] See p. 153, n. 1.　　　[2] See pp. 24, 84.

D. *The resurrection and the Messianic Kingdom*

The two biblical sources for belief in the resurrection, Isaiah 24-27 and Daniel 12, make it clear that the scene of the Messianic Kingdom is to be on this earth and that the righteous dead will be raised to take part in it. In this they are followed by several other apocalyptic writings. In I Enoch 6-36, for example, it is stated that Israel's enemies will be destroyed, despised Israel will be gathered together, and the city and the Temple will be rebuilt; then will follow the resurrection of the righteous to share with the living the blessings of the earth. They 'shall live till they beget thousands of children, and all the days of their youth and their old age shall they complete in peace' (10.17).

But there were some who could no longer consider this present world, with all its wickedness and suffering and sorrow, as a fit and proper place for the eternal Messianic Kingdom. And so, in the Similitudes of Enoch (I Enoch 37-71), for example, there is introduced the idea of a supernatural kingdom in a new heaven and a new earth, strangely united in one. 'I will transform the heaven and make it an eternal blessing and light, and I will transform the earth and make it a blessing' (45.4-5). The righteous rise from the earth in resurrection to share the bliss of this kingdom which is eternal (62.13-16).

A further development is found in the Secrets of Enoch (i.e. II Enoch) where the righteous dead rise in possession of heavenly or 'spiritual' bodies to inherit a heavenly kingdom. Paradise,[1] the final abode of the righteous, is a curious combination of the earthly and the heavenly, 'between corruptibility and incorruptibility' (8.5), wherein 'all corruptible things shall pass away' (65.10). Here the earlier idea of an earthly kingdom in which the righteous are raised in their fleshly bodies is completely absent. Over

[1] See p. 153, n. 1.

against the present material world stands the glory of the new world and the Age to Come.

The writer of II Baruch presents yet a different picture which is a compromise between the earthly and the heavenly kingdoms. What he visualizes is a temporary kingdom on earth to be followed by an eternity in heaven. Of the Messiah it is recorded, 'His principate will stand for ever, until the world of corruption is at an end' (40.3). Then will come 'the consummation of that which is corruptible, and the beginning of that which is not corruptible' (74.2). It is difficult to determine what part, if any, the righteous dead have in this Messianic Kingdom. In 30.1-2 it is stated, 'When the time of the Messiah is fulfilled, he shall return in glory. Then all who have fallen asleep in hope of him shall rise again.' Some scholars take this to refer to the Messiah's return at the close of the temporary kingdom, in which case the resurrection is to heavenly bliss where the righteous are transformed into the likeness of angels (51.10). Others take it as referring to the Messiah's coming to earth, in which case the resurrection is to a share in his earthly kingdom.

The writer of II Esdras points forward to the coming of a temporary kingdom here on this earth, to be followed by an eternity, whether on a renewed earth or in heaven itself it is hard to say. The Messiah will appear with those who have not tasted death and will dwell 400 years on the earth at the end of which he and all men will die; for the next seven 'days' the world will be turned into primaeval silence; then will take place the resurrection of all men to be brought forward for judgment at the Great Assize (cf. 7.29ff).

Out of this often confusing pattern emerges the sure and certain hope of a resurrection to eternal life, be it in an earthly Messianic Kingdom or in the glorious heaven beyond. Beneath the strange and fanciful imagery in which the picture is frequently described there lies the deep religious conviction that man is made for eternal fellowship with the living God.

2. THE NATURE OF SURVIVAL

A. *Sheol, the abode of souls*

The Old Testament picture of Sheol as the gloomy realm of the departed prevails in the two biblical apocalypses,[1] but, as as has been already indicated, some very significant changes are evident even at this early stage. No longer is Sheol the eternal abode of all who have passed through death; for some it is only an intermediate state from which at last they will be removed in the resurrection to share in the glories of the Messianic Kingdom or to receive due punishment for their sins. In both these passages, as in the Old Testament generally, the departed are described as shades or ghosts; but in the extra-biblical apocalyptic writings, even in some of the earliest of them, they are referred to as 'souls' (cf. Similitudes of Enoch, Psalms of Solomon, II Enoch, Testament of Abraham, II Esdras, II Baruch, etc.) or 'spirits' (cf. Noachic Fragments of Enoch, I Enoch 108, Assumption of Moses, II Esdras, III Baruch, etc.) which are apparently used as synonymous terms to describe the form of man's survival after death.

This development is of the utmost significance, for now the dissolution of the personal unity of body and soul (or spirit) at death no longer meant for a man the end of real personal existence as had previously been the case. We here pass from a conception of personality *wholly* dependent on body (as had been the case in Hebrew thought) to one in terms of soul or spirit which, whatever degree of physicality it carries with it,[2] is different. The degree

[1] I.e. Isa. 24-27 and Dan. 12.
[2] Even when the apocalyptists thought of the spirit or soul of the departed, they still had to think in terms of body, for this discarnate spirit or soul was believed to possess form or appearance. This is very different, however, from saying that it *has* a body in the sense in which it can be said of those spirits or souls which have taken part in the resurrection.

to which the discarnate soul or spirit is able to express personality
is a matter which will be considered later; here we note that, with
the rise of the resurrection belief, the conviction was forced upon
the apocalyptists of a continuity of this life on earth with that
in Sheol in which the departed, as conscious beings, were not
altogether cut off from the fellowship of God whose jurisdiction
was supreme even in Sheol itself.[1]

The souls or spirits of the departed not only experience consciousness, they are capable of emotional reactions. They cry
and make lamentations, being conversant with the lawless deeds
of men which are wrought on the earth (I Enoch 9.10). More
particularly they are capable of pain or pleasure in the form of
punishment or reward. The most significant passage in this
connection is II Esdras 7.[80]ff in which the writer tells how the
wicked wander in 'seven ways' or degrees of torment (7.[80])
whilst the righteous rest in 'seven orders' or dispensations of
peace (7.[91]). Their lot is that of restlessness or repose, remorse or
gratitude, fear or calm assurance. So far as their emotions or
mental processes are concerned, there would seem to be very
little difference between their capabilities in the life after death
and those which they possessed during their life upon the earth.

But taking the literature as a whole, the reader is left with the
impression that the life lived by the souls of the departed in the
intermediate abode of Sheol (or of Paradise, an extension and

---

[1] It is quite possible that the apocalyptists were influenced in their use
of the word 'soul' to describe the departed by Greek ideas of pre-existence
and immortality, particularly in II Enoch where Alexandrian influence
is evident. But it is easy to exaggerate this influence on the literature as
a whole. According to Hebrew psychology consciousness is a function not
only of the body but also of the *nephesh* which the apocalyptists came to
think of in terms of 'soul'. It is to be noted that, although frequent use is
made by Greek writers of the word *psuchai* ('souls') to describe discarnate
beings, the use of *pneumata* ('spirits') in this connection is not typically
Greek at all (cf. E. Bevan, *Symbolism and Belief*, 1938, pp. 180ff). In
certain apocalyptic writings, however, the two terms are used indiscriminately with this meaning.

specialization of the same idea) is not as full and complete as that lived upon the earth. This is seen especially in the limited nature of the soul's fellowship with God which can become complete only after the resurrection. It is still to some degree a 'shadowy life' that is lived at this intermediate stage. The souls of the departed, deprived of their bodies, must await the resurrection for their fullest expression and realization.

B. *Moral distinctions in Sheol*

One of the most significant features of the teaching of Daniel 12, marking an advance on the typically Old Testament outlook, is the fact that here for the first time in Hebrew thought moral distinctions appear between the righteous and the wicked in the life after death. At the resurrection the notably good and the notably bad are raised to receive their reward and punishment. These same distinctions are found also in the subsequent apocalyptic books, but in practically all of them they appear not simply at the time of the resurrection, but in that intermediate state immediately following death. The blessing of the righteous and the punishment of the wicked, based on moral judgments, are fully accomplished at the time of the Final Judgment, but even beforehand in Sheol there is a preliminary distribution of awards.

This fact of moral distinctions with their resulting rewards and punishments quickly led to the making of two distinct compartments or divisions in Sheol, one for the righteous and one for the wicked. This in turn led to a more pronounced and more varied distinction altering still further the topography of the life beyond, so that at length there emerged the conception of Paradise, Heaven, Hell and Gehenna in addition to Sheol itself.[1]

---

[1] The term 'Paradise' is of Persian origin and means a garden or orchard. The Greek equivalent was used by the Septuagint to translate 'the garden' of Eden. In the apocalyptic literature it signifies the abode of

In I Enoch 22, for example, three compartments are visualized, in Sheol, graded according to moral judgments already evident in the souls of the departed. In I Enoch 91-104 the writer argues strongly against the Sadducean view that in the life after death there is no difference between the fortunes of the wicked and the fortunes of the righteous. On the contrary, the wicked 'shall be wretched in great tribulation, and into darkness and chains and a burning fire where there is grievous judgment, shall their spirits enter' (103.7-8); the righteous on the other hand 'shall live and rejoice, neither shall their spirits perish' (103.4). The writer of the Testament of Abraham expresses the same belief in his picture of two gates through which the souls of men are driven: 'This narrow gate is that of the just, which leads into life, and these that enter through it enter into Paradise. For the broad gate is that of sinners, which leads to destruction and everlasting punishment' (ch. 11).[1] II Baruch records that the Final Judgment will but intensify that which the souls of the wicked have already been experiencing in Sheol (30.4-5). To such it is said, 'And now recline in anguish and rest in torment till thy last time come, in which thou wilt come again, and be tormented still more' (36.11).

It is because these moral distinctions can be made that the Final Judgment is possible. Every man will be judged according to what he has done of righteousness or of wickedness, and moral values are the criterion of judgment. In II Enoch it is stated that on that great day all the deeds of men will be weighed in the

the spirits of the righteous. It occurs three times in the New Testament (Luke 23.43; II Cor. 12.4; Rev. 2.7).

The idea of Hell as a place of torment first appears in I Enoch 22.9-13. Closely associated with it is the term 'Gehenna' which derives from the Hebrew *Ge Hinnom*, meaning 'the valley of Hinnom'. It is here that children were said to have been made to 'pass through the fire' as a sacrifice to the god Molech (cf. II Kings 16.3; Jer. 7.31, etc.). In the apocalyptic literature the term is used to describe the place of burning torment reserved for the wicked after death (cf. also Matt. 5.22; 13.42).

[1] Cf. Matt. 7.13; Luke 13.24.

balances: 'On the day of the great judgment every weight, every measure, and every makeweight will be as in the market . . . and every one shall learn his own measure, and according to his measure shall take his reward' (44.5).

c. *Moral change in the life beyond*

Some of these writers express belief in the possibility of a progressive moral change for the souls of the departed. In the Apocalypse of Moses, for example, the angels pray for the departed Adam (35.2) and the sun and the moon intercede for him (36.1). Of interest in this connection is the account given of the purification of Adam's soul (no doubt written under the influence of Greek ideas): 'Then came one of the seraphim with six wings and snatched up Adam and carried him off to the Acherusian lake, and washed him thrice, in the presence of God' (37.3). Of even greater interest is the account in the Testament of Abraham which describes how the souls of the departed undergo two tests, one by the judgment of fire and one by the judgment of the balance in which a man's good deeds are weighed over against the bad. There is pointed out to the seer an intermediate class of souls whose merits and sins are equally balanced. The prayers of the righteous on behalf of such souls may mean for them an entry into salvation (ch. 14).

The majority of these writings, however, favour the view that no change is possible once a man has departed from this life; his destiny is determined both in Sheol and at the Last Judgment by the life which he lived upon the earth. No progress is possible for the departed soul either upwards or downwards (cf. I Enoch 22). In the words of Dr Charles, Sheol becomes 'a place of petrified moralities and suspended graces'.[1] The position is made quite clear by the writer of II Baruch, 'There shall not be there again . . . change of ways, nor place for prayer, nor sending of petitions,

[1] *Op. cit.*, p. 218.

nor receiving of knowledge, nor giving of love, nor place for repentance for the soul, nor supplication for offences, nor intercession of the fathers, nor prayer of the prophets, nor help of the righteous' (85.12). Repentance will be impossible, and prayers for the dead will avail nothing.

D. *The individual soul and the Final Judgment*

In the apocalyptic Day of Final Judgment, as in the Old Testament Day of the Lord, the judgment of God sometimes takes the form of a judgment on the nations in a great crisis in history; but in the great majority of cases it assumes a definitely forensic character and takes the form of a Great Assize. Elsewhere the catastrophic and forensic types of judgment are confused, or else they are held side by side, the one representing a preliminary and the other the Final Judgment. In most cases moreover, the apocalyptists agree with the Old Testament writers, in regarding the judgment as preceding the Messianic Kingdom; but in a few cases they distinguish the kingdom from the Final Age so that the Final Judgment follows the Messianic Reign.[1]

But perhaps more significant still is the fact that here the tendency towards individualization is much more strongly pronounced. Individual souls come forward for judgment. Perhaps the clearest statement of thoroughgoing individualism is to be found in II Esdras. There it is asked whether the righteous will be able to intercede for the ungodly on the Day of Judgment, 'fathers for sons, sons for fathers, brothers for brothers, kinsfolk for their nearest, friends for their dearest' (7.[103]). In reply God says, 'The Day of Judgment is decisive . . . for then everyone shall bear his righteousness and unrighteousness' (7.[104]-[105]). At that time intercession will be fruitless, for each one must be judged by his own merits. The individual is answerable to God, and he is answerable for himself alone.

[1] See pp. 147f.

3. THE RESURRECTION BELIEF AND THE NATURE OF THE RESURRECTION BODY

A. *The resurrection of the body and the survival of personality*

We have seen that, according to the apocalyptists, the souls (or spirits) of men in Sheol were able to live an individual conscious life apart from their bodies and that in some measure at least they were able to express the personality of those who had departed from this life. But such a belief must be judged by its ultimate result and this points in almost every case to survival in the form of bodily resurrection. The souls of the departed, deprived of their bodies, were at best only 'truncated personalities' who must await the resurrection for their fullest expression. As writers in the Hebrew tradition the apocalyptists believed that personality could not be expressed *ultimately* in terms of soul (or spirit) apart from body. The Greek doctrine of immortality, though it may well have influenced their thinking concerning the after-life, could not in the end be accepted. It was utterly foreign to their Hebrew mentality, for example, to regard the souls of men as 'enclosed in the corporeal as though in a foreign hostile element, which survive the association with the body . . . distinct, complete and indivisible personalities . . . an independent substance that enters from beyond space and time into the material and perceptible world, and into external conjunction with the body, not into organic union with it'.[1] Not the immortality of the soul but the union of soul and body in resurrection, that alone could ultimately express the survival of men's personalities in the life beyond.

The soul must be united with the body, then, in resurrection because only thus could full personality be expressed. But in addition, as we have already noted, only thus could participation

---

[1] E. Rohde, *Psyche*, 1925, pp. 468-9, English Edition.

in the coming kingdom be made possible. Indeed this was the *raison d'être* of the resurrection from the dead, that the righteous might share in the kingdom. Some of the apocalyptic writers are consistent here and maintain that there should be no resurrection for the wicked; all such could not, therefore, share in the fellowship of God in the after-life or participate in the Messianic Kingdom. They appeared 'simply as disembodied souls—"naked"—in a spiritual environment without a body, without the capacity for communication with or means of expression in that environment',[1] i.e. they appeared as beings whose 'personalities' were quite inadequate to respond to the experience of participation in the kingdom or of communion with God.

Other writers, however, speak of the wicked as well as the righteous being raised up. II Baruch states that the purpose of this was to be able thereby to recognize the departed after death (50.3-4). But there is a much more cogent reason than this: it is that they might be presented before God for judgment. If men were to be adequately punished for their sins which they had committed in the body, then it was in the body that that punishment must be borne, i.e. they must be punished as men, possessing a full degree of personality, and not as truncated personalities in the form of disembodied souls. Hence it can be said of the wicked, 'Their spirit is full of lust, that they may be punished in their body ... And in proportion as the burning of their bodies becomes severe, a corresponding change shall take place in their spirit for ever and ever' (I Enoch 67.8-9).

B. *The resurrection body and its relation to its environment*

Generally speaking, according as these writers thought of the kingdom on this earth or in a supramundane state, so they thought of the resurrection body as physical or spiritual in character. In

[1] R. H. Charles, *Revelation* (International Critical Commentary), 1920, vol. 2, pp. 193-4.

those writings where the kingdom is to be established on the earth, comparatively little is said regarding the actual nature of the resurrection body, but in each case it is clearly implied that a physical body like that of men in this present life is intended (cf. Isaiah 26, Dan. 12, I Enoch 10.17, etc.). This idea is most frequently found in the earliest of these writings, but it is not confined to these. In the Sibylline Oracles we read, 'Then God himself shall fashion again the bones and ashes of men, and shall raise up mortals once more as they were before' (Bk. IV, lines 181-182). This belief in a physical resurrection may perhaps be best illustrated by reference to a writing which is not classed among the apocalyptic books, but which in this respect reflects the belief expressed there. In II Macc. 14.46 we read of one Razis that, 'his blood now drained from him, he tore out his bowels, taking both his hands to them, and flung them at the crowds. So he died, calling on him who is the Lord of life and spirit to restore them to him again'. Elsewhere the same writer tells how the third of the seven martyred brothers stretched forth his hands and said, 'These I had from heaven; for his name's sake, I count them nought; from him I hope to get them back again' (7.11).

The transference of man's after-life from earth to heaven, however, led inevitably to belief in a 'spiritual' body which corresponded to its heavenly environment. In the Similitudes of Enoch, where there is a curious mingling of earth and heaven in which angels and men live together (39.4-5), 'the righteous and elect . . . shall have been clothed with garments of glory. And there shall be the garments of life from the Lord of Spirits' (62.15-16). The 'garments of glory', as we shall see, are the 'spiritual' resurrection bodies of the righteous. At the close of the Messianic Kingdom, recorded in II Baruch, the righteous are to be raised to dwell in heaven itself (51.10). Although they are to be raised from the dust of the earth (42.8) in their physical bodies with no change in their appearance (50.2), there takes place after the judgment a gradual transformation until the physical bodies are changed into 'spiritual' bodies (ch. 51; cf. also II Enoch 22.8-9).

c. *The relation of the 'spiritual' body to the physical body*

It is customary for the 'spiritual' resurrection body to be described in several of these books under the figure of 'garments' of light or glory. In II Enoch 22.8, for example, Michael is bidden, 'Go and take Enoch out of his earthly garments . . . and put him into the garments of my glory', i.e. Enoch's earthly body is to be replaced by a heavenly body, prepared beforehand, like those of the angels of God (22.9f).

Different though they are, there is yet a curious connection between the physical body and the 'spiritual' body which defies explanation. In the Apocalypse of Moses the body of Adam is buried in the earthly Paradise (38.5), and yet God says to the archangels, 'Go away to Paradise in the third heaven, and strew linen clothes and cover the body of Adam, and bring oil of the "oil of fragrance" and pour it over him' (40.2). And so 'they prepared him for burial' (40.2). The connection here between the body on earth and the body in the heavenly Paradise is not made clear, but it would seem that the latter is a counterpart of the former and that it is this heavenly body which awaits the resurrection. Not only is it a counterpart of the physical body, it is co-existent with it until the day of the resurrection (II Enoch 22.8).

Elsewhere the 'spiritual' body is a transformed physical body (cf. I Enoch 108.11); the body which is buried in the earth will be raised up 'a glorious body' on the day of resurrection.[1] The

---

[1] Cf. I Cor. 15.42ff: 'It is sown in dishonour, it is raised in glory; it is sown in weakness, it is raised in power; it is sown a natural body, it is raised a spiritual body'.

writer of II Baruch asks concerning those who are to be resurrected, 'Will they then resume this form of the present, and put on these entrammelling members . . . or wilt thou perchance change these things that have been in the world as also the world?' (49.3).[1] He is told that at the resurrection the bodies of the wicked and the righteous alike will be raised with no change in their form or appearance (50.2), making possible the recognition of those who have died (50.3-4).[2] When the judgment is passed the bodies of men will be gradually transformed in a series of changes into 'spiritual' bodies.

The 'spiritual' body of Enoch, we are told, needs no food or anything earthly for its satisfaction (II Enoch 56.2) and as such is like those of the angels; and yet when he returns to earth for a space of thirty days, presumably in his heavenly body (though his face had to be 'frozen' so that men could behold him; cf. 37.2), not only is he recognized by his friends, but he even allows the whole assembly to approach and kiss him (64.2-3).[3]

The 'spiritual' body, then, is not merely a symbolic body in the sense that it is representational, simply representing the earthly body but being something quite different in identity from it, having no organic relation with it; rather it may be described as constitutive, for it is constituted by body as men understand that term and has the same substructure, however much the concept is spiritualized. The 'spiritual' body is the physical body transformed so as to correspond to that environment which is natural to the nature and being of God himself.

---

[1] Cf. I Cor. 15.35: 'How are the dead raised up? And with what body do they come?' The account of the transformation of the resurrection body in II Baruch 49-51 finds a striking parallel in I Corinthians 15.

[2] Cf. Mark 9.43ff which refers to the survival of physical deformities in the life after death.

[3] Cf. John 20.27 for the physical properties of the resurrection body of Jesus.

The apparent contradiction between the 'spiritual' body as a transformed physical body and as its heavenly counterpart, co-existent with it till the day of resurrection, is partly resolved by the belief that the 'spiritual' body grows *pari passu* with the physical body and that a man's righteous acts performed in the body of flesh condition the fashioning of the body in heaven. This belief is expressed explicitly in the Christian apocalyptic writings,[1] and implicitly in the Jewish. 'This spiritual body', writes Dr Charles,[2] 'is the joint result of God's grace and man's faithfulness. It is, on the one hand, a divine gift. . . . On the other hand, the spiritual body is in a certain sense the present possession of the faithful, and can, therefore, only be possessed through faithfulness.' Man is created 'from invisible and from visible nature; of both are his death and life' (II Enoch 30.10). And both are the creation of God.

---

[1] Cf. Rev. 3.4: 'But thou hast a few names in Sardis which did not defile their garments: and they shall walk with me in white, for they are worthy.' Cf. also 16.15.

That the 'spiritual' body is already one with the person for whom it is prepared is made clear in the Syriac 'Hymn of the Soul' which reads, 'I saw the garment made like unto me as it had been in a mirror. And I beheld upon it all myself, and I knew and saw myself through it, that we were divided asunder, being of one, and again were one in one shape.' (cf. M. R. James, *The Apocryphal New Testament*, 1924, p. 414).

[2] *Op. cit.*, vol. I, pp. 187-188.

A Select Bibliography

History and Religion

E. R. Bevan, *Jerusalem under the High Priests* (Arnold, 1904).

F. F. Bruce, *Second Thoughts on the Dead Sea Scrolls* (Paternoster, 1956).

F. C. Burkitt, *Jewish and Christian Apocalypses* (Oxford, 1914).

Millar Burrows, *The Dead Sea Scrolls* (Secker and Warburg, 1956).

R. H. Charles, *Religious Development between the Old and the New Testaments* (Home University Library, 1914).

Clarendon Bible: G. H. Box, *Judaism in the Greek Period* (Oxford, 1932).

W. R. Farmer, *Maccabees, Zealots and Josephus* (Columbia, 1956).

G. F. Moore, *Judaism in the First Centuries of the Christian Era*, 3 vols. (Cambridge, Mass., 1927-30).

R. H. Pfeiffer, *History of New Testament Times, with an Introduction to the Apocrypha* (New York, Harper, 1949; now, A. & C. Black).

H. W. Robinson, *The History of Israel* (Duckworth, 1938).

N. H. Snaith, *The Jews from Cyrus to Herod* (The Religious Education Press, Ltd, 1949).

The Apocryphal Literature

R. H. Charles, ed. by, *The Apocrypha and Pseudepigrapha of the Old Testament*, 2 vols. (Oxford, 1913).

R. T. Herford, *Talmud and Apocrypha* (Soncino Press, 1933).

Bruce M. Metzger, *An Introduction to the Apocrypha* (Oxford, 1957).

H. H. Rowley, *The Relevance of Apocalyptic* (Lutterworth Press, 1944).

H. H. Rowley, *Jewish Apocalyptic and the Dead Sea Scrolls* (The Athlone Press, 1957).

R. H. Pfeiffer—as above. See also a good short introduction in *The Apocrypha according to the Authorized Version, with an introduction by Robert H. Pfeiffer* (New York, Harper, 1953), and in *The Interpreter's Bible*, vol. 1 (New York, Abingdon-Cokesbury Press; now, Thomas Nelson and Sons).

Fuller references will be found in the footnotes throughout the book.

Rulers and Events

Ptolemies and Seleucids in Palestine

Ptolemies in control of Palestine	B.C. 312-198
Ptolemy I (Soter I)	312-283
Ptolemy II (Philadelphos)	285-247
Ptolemy III (Euergetes I)	247-221
Ptolemy IV (Philopator)	221-203
Ptolemy V (Epiphanes)	203-181

(The Ptolemaic rule continued till 30 B.C. when Egypt became a Roman province.)

Seleucids in control of Palestine	198-143
Antiochus III (The Great)	223-187
Seleucus IV (Philopator)	187-175
Antiochus IV (Epiphanes)	175-163
Antiochus V (Eupator)	163-162
Demetrius I (Soter)	162-150
Alexander Balas	150-145
Demetrius II (Nicator)	145-138
	and 129-125

(The Seleucid rule continued till 64 B.C. when it was brought to an end by Pompey.)

Maccabees and Hasmoneans

Judas Maccabaeus	B.C. 166-160
Jonathan (High Priest)	160-143
Simon (High Priest)	142-134

John Hyrcanus I (High Priest)	B.C. 134-104
Aristobulus I (High Priest and King)	103-102
Alexander Jannaeus (High Priest and King)	102-76
Alexandra Salome	75-67
Hyrcanus II (High Priest)	75-66
	and 63-40
Aristobulus II (High Priest and King)	66-63
Antigonus (High Priest and King)	40-37
Herod the Great	37-4

Rulers in Judaea from the death of Herod to the Jewish War

Archelaus	4 B.C.-A.D. 6
Roman procurators	A.D. 6-41
Herod Agrippa I	41-44
Roman procurators	44-66

Important Events

Temple polluted by Antiochus Epiphanes	B.C. 168
The Maccabean Revolt	167
Rededication of the Temple	165
Jonathan appointed High Priest	152
Independence granted	142
Simon appointed hereditary High Priest and Ethnarch	141
Accession of John Hyrcanus I and the emergence of the Pharisees and Sadducees	134-104
Independence lost: Pompey captures Jerusalem	63
Accession of Herod	37
Death of Herod	4
The Jewish War	A.D. 66-70
Jerusalem destroyed by Titus	70

Index of Subjects

Index of Texts

A. THE OLD TESTAMENT

B. THE APOCRYPHAL BOOKS

c. THE NEW TESTAMENT